The Queer Tarot Guidebook

Ash + Chess

RP STUDIO
PHILADELPHIA

RP Studio™
Hachette Book Group
1290 Avenue of the Americas, New York, NY 10104
www.runningpress.com
@Running_Press

Printed in China

First Edition: April 2022

Published by RP Studio, an imprint of Perseus Books, LLC, a subsidiary of Hachette Book Group, Inc. The RP Studio name and logo is a trademark of the Hachette Book Group.

Design by Jenna McBride

ISBN: 978-0-7624-7488-2

APS

Contents

Introduction

Welcome to *The Queer Tarot Guidebook*, a tool we hope guides you on your path to self-discovery and self-love. Tarot is a wonderful way to explore how you perceive the world around you and the situations you face in your day-to-day life, and we thought it only necessary that the queer community have a deck that focuses on the trials and tribulations we face living our truth every day. In a world where trans people are consistently stripped of their rights and endangered, queer couples are discriminated against in family planning, and fatal hate crimes continue to happen without justice—queer people need a safe space and something to turn to when things get really ugly. While this deck can't fix the injustices forced upon the queer community by the outside world, we hope it can be a guiding light for inner growth and strength for queers everywhere.

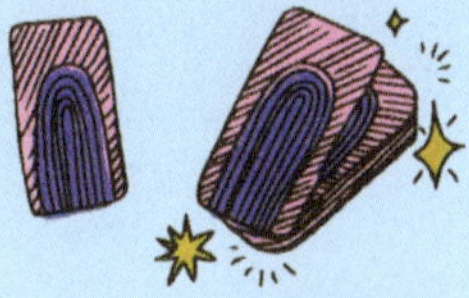

Ash here! I first truly discovered the beauty and significance of reading tarot through our friend Amber Berkins while we still lived in Brooklyn, only a few years ago! Chess and I went to Amber's apartment, around the corner from ours in Bedford-Stuyvesant, for a small gathering of friends for a New Moon party. Amber read tarot for each of us and led meditation and journaling, all while creating and cultivating a safe space for everyone to become vulnerable and open. I was afraid at first to have my cards read, and I was actually dreading it leading up to the party. Our friend Caitlin went first and without even knowing what her reading was about going in, we all could see the inner and outer workings of what was going on in her life that the cards were bringing to light. It was such a wild thing to watch, the power of these cards being pulled out and spread around the room. After seeing Amber at work, deciphering and interpreting the spread, I decided to go next. It was my first tarot reading ever, and it was about my mom and our relationship. After the reading was through, I was in complete awe. Amber was able to intuit and advise, all through this plastic-coated paper deck of cards, all while not even knowing what my problems and fears were up front. The reading opened my eyes in a way I hadn't ever imagined could happen. I was hooked.

My entire life I had adamantly avoided tarot, psychics, fortune-tellers, and the works, all because the Southern Baptist Christian religion I grew up in grouped all of these things together and taught me that they were essentially a gateway to hell, organized and led by the devil themself. It would be an understatement to say I didn't actually know what tarot was. Many people have this same twisted misconception about what tarot actually is. The church frames tarot in such a forbidden light because of what the cards actually encourage: enlightenment, self-discovery, intuition, and self-empowerment, among many other concepts that organized religion often likes to suppress.

Shortly after Amber read my cards at that New Moon party, I gained the courage to purchase my first deck—the initial step in really diving into the world of tarot and a really bold move on my part, given my prior extreme and unfounded fear of tarot. All my life, I had been drawn to the artwork on the cards, the mysticism of it all, yet I had been too afraid and too overwhelmed with the thought of getting into it. Beneath this fear, I always dreamed of illustrating an entire deck someday. It always felt like a distant dream, too big to fulfill, too scary to actually conquer. I started diving into meanings with my new deck, pulling a card a day, Googling interpretations from different decades and different readers. I finally began to understand what practicing tarot actually entails and the benefits that can come from it.

Chess here! Like Ash, I got my first experience with tarot at Amber's house. I'm more of a skeptic, so I went in doubting I would leave the space with any insight I didn't already have. I asked a very general question, and I recall being impressed by Amber's reading but still thinking to myself, "Maybe my question was just *that* vague!" Ash got more into it and always wanted to practice reading spreads with me. I begrudgingly complied, but didn't really ever feel like fully committing. In February 2019, my beloved dog Boomer was diagnosed with cancer and he began to deteriorate before my eyes. It became obvious, quickly, that he wasn't happy. I realized I was going to have

to make a choice on when to put him down and end his suffering. I contacted a house-call vet and scheduled a time for them to come. It felt surreal and wrong to plan to end my sweet dog's life. Ash had been pulling a card a day the whole time he was sick. I remember when the day came for Boomer to be put down, I pulled The World. The end of the Fool's Journey traced in the Major Arcana. It felt like the right card for the moment and, for me, it affirmed my belief that I made the right choice for my sweet pup.

This moment just showed me what tarot really is—it's what you make of it. It's ever changing. If I pulled The World tomorrow, it would mean something completely different. If I pulled it in a spread in relation to other cards, the meaning changes yet again. It's this acknowledgment that holds the real power of the tarot—the idea of using universal themes like loss, grief, achievement, belonging, and exploration in order to better navigate these situations as they come up in life. Time and time again, the tarot cards show you what you need. Whether it's finding your identity, seeking help in a time of crisis, or wondering what steps to take next—the tarot serves as a guide to better understand yourself and your journey.

We both came out as queer way before we knew what tarot actually consisted of, but had we known that a stack of cards could've made coming to terms with who we are a tad bit easier, we both would've picked up the tarot in a heartbeat.

This *Queer Tarot* deck was made with all queers in mind—all identities, all body types, all races, all ethnicities, all abilities, all sexualities, all people. And since we wanted this deck to be as inclusive as our resources would allow, we were able to cast real live queer folx from all over the world to be a part of the cards. And let me tell you from experience, queer people are the cutest people. Without Amber, without our queer models, and without the people who continue to expand queer visibility in society, we wouldn't be here and this deck wouldn't exist. We're so glad that it does, and we hope that it changes your life, even if in the smallest of ways.

♥, Ash + Chess

Queerness and Tarot

Why are queerness and the practice of tarot so relevant to one another? Like humanity itself, tarot decks have evolved in their meanings, interpretations, and symbolism over the course of many years. The tarot is a tool that has grown and changed through many generations, much like the ever-changing collective understanding of the queer experience. Incorporating queer experiences into tarot, making it more inclusive for a greater number of people, is one of the many ways we can continue to normalize the LGBTQ+ community. As a practice, tarot helps you find yourself, which is something everyone in the queer community can use a hand with in this very heteronormative world.

The illustrations and interpretations revolving around gender and sexuality are key aspects of this deck. Just because one gender identity is represented on a certain card doesn't mean your reading or understanding of that card should exclude all the other gender identities or sexualities that are out there. This is especially important to remember with the traditionally named "Queen" and "King" Court cards, as well as the outwardly gendered

Major Arcana cards, such as the Emperor or High Priestess. Gender and sexuality are fluid and socially constructed, as are the many interpretations of each and every tarot card. When using this deck, embrace a more open worldview, and let the harmful and restricting gender binaries melt away.

Something most queer people have in common is that we do not typically conform to societal standards when it

comes to our gender identities and sexualities. Being queer can be a risky and struggle-filled journey for many—one that can be made even harder depending on where in the world you live. In many countries, the ability to be out and proud is nonexistent; in the United States, this privilege is growing, but being queer in America is still extremely dangerous for so many. Some of the laws that police queer bodies may initially appear to be laxer, even progressive, but queer people in the U.S. still fall victim to hate crimes nearly every day, and laws are still being passed to erase the queer community. Around the world, there is an epidemic of violence and murder perpetrated against Black trans women; sex workers are punished and arrested for merely doing their jobs; queer children are kicked out of their homes; conversion therapy is forced upon young queers; intersex infants are forced through surgery into binary gender identities, trans athletes are being banned from playing sports . . . the list goes on. Homophobia and transphobia are real things the queer community faces every day. You may or may not find yourself in any of these situations, but we all must remember as a community that no one is free until we are all free.

By utilizing tarot in your everyday queer life, you can begin to build a strong and loving relationship with yourself, as well as with your community. Getting to know ourselves as queer people and learning to understand our deepest desires and dreams can be the key to understanding the world around us a little better. This is an important gift we give ourselves—something we may not have had or realized the importance of in the past. Let the *Queer Tarot* deck be a guide in navigating your queerness to its fullest extent and a source of strength and curiosity as you grow more open to getting to know yourself.

The Artwork

The artwork in this deck was inspired by and adapted from the 1909 Smith-Rider-Waite deck, one of the most well-known tarot decks of the past century and a set that remains incredibly popular today. Originally illustrated by Pamela Colman Smith, each card is packed with symbolism that can still be applied to today's tarot readings. With the *Queer Tarot* cards, we've essentially revamped the classic by illustrating as many kinds of queer people as we could fit into the deck. These real, diverse queers stand in place of the traditional white and skinny figures portrayed in the original. Representation of the queer community is something that can always be expanded on, so we are very excited to provide a queer-inclusive deck that features different identities, genders, body types, sexualities, races, abilities, and more.

Each card in your deck features a real-life queer person! The model's name and pronouns can be found alongside each card's description. We felt that the only way we could really capture the queer community's beauty and essence was to illustrate actual people who are living their truths in their own personal ways every day.

These cards are extra special because all of the original artwork was printed on a risograph. Risograph machines are these wild duplicators from Japan that look like clunky copier machines you would find in an office. They were originally intended for mass printing in single colors, like for flyers or letters. Within the past decade or so, riso-printing has taken an artful turn and is now evolving into a wonderful and experimental new way to produce art, using soy-based inks, some of which are fluorescent or metallic. Each card was designed and set up with CMYK separation, with each color layer printed separately. For those riso freaks out there, the colors we printed with are made from combinations that included Sunflower Yellow, Light Lime, Fluorescent Pink, Fluorescent Orange, Aqua, Cornflower Blue, and Black on an RZ 360 UI. In order to get all of these brilliant colors into the deck when printing just four or five hues per card, many of the colors were trapped, creating a new color when printed over one another.

A lot of work was not only put into this deck through design, but through manual labor as well, and we enjoyed every second of it. We chose to risograph this entire deck because the imperfections and natural textures and brilliance that come with risograph art seem to embody the concept of life itself—it's not always going to be perfect, and there will be times where your life feels like it's colored outside of the lines, but that doesn't mean it isn't beautiful.

How to Handle

This deck is your new baby! Treat it with love and respect. The positive energy you give will make your bond with your deck stronger and more meaningful. Take care of it like it's the most valuable thing in your world. It's always nice to set up rituals using your deck, like washing your hands before handling it, reading your cards in a quiet and peaceful setting where you feel comfortable, and giving them all of your attention when they are out of their protective case. And don't leave them strewn about the floor or on the table unattended—because the dog will eat them, you will spill coffee on them, or the cat will swipe them off the table and onto the floor. Use your deck for yourself, with friends or family, or with whomever you feel comfortable in sharing the reading experience. This deck is meant as a tool to learn more about yourself all while posing questions to help you discover and explore ideas and concepts that you may have never considered. Using the *Queer Tarot* deck should be a positive learning experience, even when you come across cards that might seem negative. Employ your readings as a way to look inward. As time goes by, you will develop a deeper understanding with your deck, as it opens your eyes to new possibilities and helps you grow into an even more authentic version of yourself.

Shuffling the Cards

Each time you do a reading, you should shuffle your cards. This gives you some personal one-on-one time with them, allowing your energy to pass into the cards for the reading. You can shuffle however you would like, but it is best to be gentle with the cards. You can mix them up on a clean surface and then put them all back together or cut the deck in half and distribute every few cards to the top and bottom, back and forth. Do what feels right to you, and shuffle while thinking about your question or the topic you are doing a reading about.

Once you feel that you have shuffled the cards enough, cut the deck into three separate piles, letting the natural breaks choose where you divide it. Pick a pile, then put the piles back together into one stack, with your chosen stack on the top. Now you are ready to pull your cards.

A Note on Reverse Meanings

A reverse description is considered when you pull a card upside down. They typically shed light on the other side of the card, meaning that they can often reveal a negative or opposite idea of the card's upright meaning.

Not all readers, especially those new to the practice of reading tarot, are comfortable utilizing reverse meanings right off the bat—and that's okay! If you're not quite there yet, you can shuffle your cards while keeping them all in the upright position, or as you pull them, display them upright if they have been mixed up. Reverse meanings can help give you more perspective on a card when performing a reading, and even when you are reading without reversals, simply reading the description can give deeper insight.

Choosing a Spread

A *spread* refers to the order in which you lay your tarot cards, with each card position representing a different aspect of your reading. There are tons of fun and different ways to pull spreads, and each one typically focuses on a specific type of situation. Often, you will have a specific question or focus in mind for your reading, which can help you narrow down which arrangement to use.

When it comes to choosing a spread for a reading, think about what makes the most sense for the situation you are currently in or what is most relevant to your question. If you have a topic weighing on your heart or mind and you don't know which spread to pick to address it, read through the descriptions below until one clicks with you. Your intuition will tell you when you've found the one you need. And the fun thing about spreads is that there are endless options listed online or in other guidebooks, and you can even make up your own!

SPECTRUM SPREAD

A classic spread in tarot is a simple three-card option, with the cards representing the past, present, and future. The Spectrum Spread draws on that traditional formulation, but with a little something extra for each card you will pull. In this six-card spread, you can navigate the past, present, and future with a reflection card for each, lending you deeper insight.

USES queer identity, coming out, exploration of self/sexuality, generally all things queer

1. **Past feelings**
2. **Struggles**
3. **Present feelings**
4. **Hopes/desires**
5. **Future potential**
6. **Action**

IDENTITY SPREAD

The Identity Spread is a simple three-card spread that is intended to help you pinpoint what might be holding you back from living to your fullest potential at this moment in time. Whether you are questioning your gender identity, your sexuality, or even your beliefs, this spread can be a simple way to start unpacking those feelings.

USES when you feel stuck, when you lose sight of yourself, when you don't know who you are, coming out

1. **Who you are now/how you see yourself**
2. **What is keeping you there**
3. **Who you want to be**

CHESSIE'S GOOD MOOD SPREAD

Similar to the Identity Spread, Chessie's Good Mood Spread helps you uncover a difficult issue you may be dealing with, how to reflect on that issue, and how to take action as you move forward. This spread is great for when you're feeling down and want to get out of that rut you've been sulking in for so long.

USES when you're feeling doubtful of yourself or unconfident

1. **Issue at hand**
2. **Reflection on issue**
3. **Action**
4. **Reflection on action**

NEW RELATIONSHIP SPREAD

The exciting part about the New Relationship Spread is that *new* and *relationship* are relative to the specific situation. This spread is meant for literally any type of relationship—it is all about however you define the term *relationship*. *New* is also up to your interpretation—it doesn't have to be limited to people you just met. This spread is all about connection, whatever that may mean to you.

USES

exploring dynamics in any relationship, next steps, connection to people, entering a new relationship

1. **Purpose/overall vibe**
2. **You/what you offer/what you bring**
3. **Them/what they offer (if more than one person or partner is involved, you can build off of position 3 for each person)**
4. **What to leave behind**

ASH'S NEW PERSPECTIVE SPREAD

This four-card spread is divided into two sections: the first card represents your situation at hand, and cards two, three, and four represent new perspectives to consider. How do these contributing cards weave into your story? Are they telling you things you already know or exposing a new source of clarity? This spread is best used when you are feeling stuck, looking for more information, or just want to clear things up.

USES new perspective, clarity, feeling at a standstill, decision-making

1. **Situation or concern**
2. **New perspective**
3. **New perspective**
4. **New perspective**

DESIRE SPREAD

This two-card spread is a simple yet deeply insightful way to uncover truths and what is keeping them hidden, whether from you or the world around you. The first card represents your truest desire, something you ache for and something you want, and the second card represents your roadblock: the thing that is keeping you from living out your dreams. This spread comes in handy even in the tiniest of situations. Not only is it a discovery spread, it is also a spread that encourages reflection on the things we want and why we desire them so badly.

USES facing a roadblock, feeling unproductive, next steps for reaching a goal, coming to terms with loss

1. **Your desires**
2. **What's keeping you from what you want**

GOALS SPREAD

The Goals Spread is a five-card spread that helps you set up a game plan for how to reach a desired outcome. When working toward a goal, a lot of factors are at play. This spread is divided up into four points of action to help you map out how to get where you want to go!

USES goal setting, achievement, self-growth, habit making or breaking

1. **Goal**
2. **What to work on**
3. **What to avoid**
4. **Physical action**
5. **Mental action**

Intuition

Intuition is an extremely important part of reading tarot. Intuition is most easily equated to the "gut feeling" you get when something seems off, or when something seems just right. It's that unconscious instinct inside of you. Unlocking your intuition and reading tarot cards go hand in hand, because in order to get the most out of the cards, you have to dive into the depths of your mind and heart. Practicing tarot often reveals the truths that we are searching for or are hiding from. And being honest with yourself and allowing your intuition to lead will do you a lot of good and help you find what you are looking for.

The Deck

The 78-card tarot deck is typically divided into two sections: the Major Arcana, which consists of archetypal cards, and the Minor Arcana, which is divided into numbered "pip" cards and court cards.

Major Arcana

The Major Arcana is made up of 22 cards, each featuring common characters, themes, and archetypes that we might find within our psyche. The cards in this group are often considered to be the main idea of a reading.

Minor Arcana

The Minor Arcana is made up of 56 cards, divided into four suits, each with its own set of court cards. The cards in the Minor Arcana typically represent details and goings-on in your everyday life, acting as the small support system to the Major Arcana's big themes. The four suits are Wands, Cups, Swords, and Pentacles.

Pip Cards

The pip cards of the deck are comprised of Ace through 10 in each of the four suits and constitute the bulk of the Minor Arcana. These cards usually represent situations, adding a little more depth and clarity in your readings.

Court Cards

There are four court cards in each suit of the Minor Arcana:

the Page, the Knight, the Queen, and the King. These cards depict people but can be read three different ways: as a person, as a situation, or as yourself. They make up the remainder of the Minor Arcana alongside the pip cards.

Wands

Ruled by Fire. The suit of Wands represents inspiration and creativity, ambitions, goals, hopes and dreams, and everything in between. This suit is connected to your mind and spirit, in the sense that the ideas and goals Wands represent are not yet present in tangible form. As a suit that is ruled by fire, the Wands ultimately deal with things you are passionate about, as well as your truths.

Cups

Ruled by Water. The suit of Cups deals with emotions, relationships, human connection, love, friendship, and all matters of the heart. Cups often represent platonic, romantic, and familial connections with the people in your life, as well as the many emotions that you can feel in every possible situation. Your heart

commands this suit. As a suit that is ruled by water, Cups encourage fluidity in all aspects of your life.

Swords

Ruled by Air. The suit of Swords covers action, intellect, conflict, and power. It is associated with turmoil and distress, as this is a battle-like suit. But like all suits, Swords possesses both positives and negatives. As a suit that is ruled by air, Swords often come up when you need a little push through to the other side, or, in other words, a path to overcoming.

Pentacles

Ruled by Earth. The suit of Pentacles represents worldly and material possessions, including home matters, money, career, greed, and generosity. It also covers the things in our lives that have sentimental value, like family (chosen or otherwise), friends, and personal growth. As a suit that is ruled by earth, Pentacles symbolize stability.

Card Meanings

Tarot has been around for centuries, and as a result, interpretations of the cards are bound to evolve—indeed, many already have. Our descriptions in this guidebook have been adapted from those who came before us. We've also sought out the help of professional tarot readers working today. With that said, if you long to dive deeper into the world of tarot card meanings, there are tons of different interpretations out there. If you're not quite feeling fulfilled with the meanings we suggest here, don't hesitate to explore other ways in which a specific card can be understood! It all comes down to your own intuition when reading your cards.

In each card description, you will find keywords that summarize the theme of the card along with a list of questions and actions that you can implement in your life to live in the energy that the card brings. A description of the artwork and queer symbols expressed in each card can be found in the back of the book.

0
The Fool

I
The Magician

The High Priestess

III
The Empress

IV
The Emperor

V
The Hierophant

VI
The Lovers

VII
The Chariot

VIII
Strength

IX
The Hermit

X
Wheel of Fortune

XI
Justice

Major Arcana

The Fool, 0

SPONTANEITY, OPTIMISM, INNOCENCE

The Fool is the very first card in the Major Arcana, symbolizing the beginning of a long and fruitful journey. This start can be particularly scary at times, just like the anxiety of coming out to a new set of folx. However, the essence of this card embodies the innocence and naivete we possess as humans, and the very authentic and delicate root of your soul. It presents a choice to indulge your desires and embark on your wildest dreams without hesitation. What does your soul ache for? The Fool usually indicates stepping into a world in which you are lacking experience but ready to spring forward anyway. Your optimism will protect you in these untested waters and will block out all the fear and doubts that usually come with beginning something new and hard. This brand-new journey is ready for you, and your raw desire and inspiration will fuel the first leg. A new beginning or just completely starting over is a great thing! It gives you the opportunity to learn about the task at hand, as well as yourself. Keep holding on to the blind passion the Fool brings out in you. It will get you far.

REVERSE: The Fool appears in reverse when you are being naive when starting a project. Remember to have foresight and a vision to direct you where to go; otherwise you will feel like you're lacking any forward movement!

THINGS TO CONSIDER: Do something you have always wanted to do! What is something you wish to learn on this new journey? Is there a dream you have always wanted to live but haven't had the courage to start?

MODELS: Alett — they/she; Lana — dog

The Magician, I

CONFIDENCE, PASSION, SELF-EMPOWERMENT

The Magician marks the beginning of something beautiful and powerful—all made possible by the magic that lies within you. It is pretty much the go-ahead for whatever big dreams you've got on your mind right now. It's time to use your potential and passion to manifest your goals, within the realm of possibility. All four elements—fire, water, wind, and earth—are within the Magician's reach right now, so use this as a reminder to keep balance while executing your endeavors. The Magician can also represent the emergence of confidence in your life as a queer person. As part of a marginalized community, confidence and self-empowerment may be harder to come by since queers often encounter negativity and disapproval of our identities. Self-empowerment and pride are two essential things that help the queer community thrive. If you aren't able to access either in your life, use this time to work toward embracing these things for yourself and for your community. Now is a better time than ever to harness the magic inside of you and use it to do great things!

REVERSE: **Maybe you feel hesitant about taking a step toward something new, like you haven't planned enough to get started. You want everything to be lined up and perfectly in place before starting to chase this dream. However, the Magician is reminding you to stay alert for any small opportunities—maybe they're building blocks to your goal. Maybe you have started on your big, lifelong project, but you're feeling like you aren't making enough progress or feeling successful. The Magician can also be a sign that your goal is wholly self-involved—you're working too much on your personal gain. Focus on your higher Self**

and what your purpose is. Are your goals helping you reach that purpose?

THINGS TO CONSIDER: What are your big dreams and goals right now? Are your goals realistic for yourself and your resources? Take stock of what's available to you and how you can use it to make progress in your endeavors. Consider focusing on one thing and put all of your energy and efforts into that, rather than a bunch of different projects all at once.

MODEL: Jul — they/them

The High Priestess, II

SUBCONSCIOUS MIND, NURTURING, REST, FEMININITY

The High Priestess is radical and mysterious, offering you spiritual enlightenment and wisdom. They are a muse, able to travel between the conscious and subconscious mind and encouraging you to switch between these two realms. The High Priestess often symbolizes femininity, an energy everyone holds—intuition, rest, reflection, and divine wisdom. Connect deeply with this—you know your own truth better than anybody else, and the High Priestess reminds you of this, no matter what anyone else may say. Take a moment to step back and see which parts of your life seem to lack balance, and make the time to explore deep within yourself to find equilibrium. Remember, you are a part of a community and the High Priestess prompts you to step back and collaborate with others rather than work against them. This card reminds you to take a deep breath and be still. Your mind, or pressure from others, may be hounding you to make snap decisions or judgments, but the High Priestess encourages you to explore stillness and instead consider the big picture. This card may appear when you're facing a situation in which you *must* make a decision but truly feel you don't have all the necessary information. If this is the case, go with your gut and trust your instincts.

REVERSE: You may be feeling blocked or closed off to your feminine nature, like you need to act and execute rather than ponder. Take the time to practice your intuition and begin to trust yourself again. Rest.

THINGS TO CONSIDER: Meditate and enjoy the calm that comes with it. Explore the feelings and thoughts passing through you.

MODEL: Chala. — they/he

The Empress, III

CONNECTION, SELF-LOVE, UNCONDITIONAL LOVE, ABUNDANCE

The energy of the Empress is generous and giving—they may represent your support system or are perhaps an indication that you are someone else's. The Empress is in a place of thriving, surrounded by abundance and luxury. They hold an energy of a devoted parent—unconditional love, ultimately nurturing, and full of compassion. This type of energy blooms from connection—to people, animals, and all living things. Pulling this card is a nudge to let yourself be loving and kind. Self-love and self-care are big practices for the Empress as well. Embrace these practices yourself, and channel all the loving you can. This card can also be a suggestion to shift directions if you're feeling disconnected or uninspired. The Empress sees the world as a beautiful, cohesive, and magical place.

REVERSE: You are a caregiver and devote most, if not all, of your time to taking care of others. When the Empress appears reversed, this card is asking you to prioritize some self-love before you begin to feel resentful of those you spend so much time caring about. Consider coming up with some self-love rituals—a nightly warm bath, some candle lighting, some alone time. Put yourself first every now and then!

THINGS TO CONSIDER: Call a friend or make plans to hang out with someone. Take a moment to thank the support system in your life, or make some time to think about the support you give to people. Go outside and just hang out with nature. Let it change your perspective.

MODEL: jae — they/them

The Emperor, IV

STRUCTURE, POWER, ACTION

The Emperor represents a figure who is in charge and unafraid of conflict, as long as it leads to a solution. You have used your logic and wisdom to build structures, and others see you as stable and secure. People often see the Emperor as someone they can lean on and trust. They have no fear of what others may say and command respect from those around them. They don't get caught up in emotions—there's no time for that—but rather seek to think logically and come to a resolution. This card encourages you to be direct with your feelings and needs rather than seeking a passive-aggressive approach. It asks you to be protective and put your needs first, callous as that may sound. They remind you to protect yourself and those who are close to you, and to stick up for yourself when it matters. At times, the Emperor can serve as a reminder to pass on your leadership qualities to others and give them a chance too, so that they can one day be as powerful and confident as you are. The appearance of the Emperor can also mean that although you may not feel powerful, you have gained the attention of someone that is—a boss, a mentor, etc. If you haven't been feeling so strong, the Emperor reminds you that this feeling won't last forever and that you will rise out of this dark period in your life.

REVERSE: You may be abusing the authority that others give you. Reflect on your relationship to power. Are you sharing it?

Are you helping others grow into leaders as well? Consider your own relationship to your authority—do you need to be rigid all the time, or could you become more flexible? Let down your armor and open up.

THINGS TO CONSIDER: Who is controlling your life right now? You or someone/something else? Even though you are powerful, don't let it go to your head. You can guide others to discover their own power too. Stand up for yourself and your community. Remember, too much power consolidated in one person or place is not a good thing.

MODEL: Taylor Tucker — he/him

The Hierophant, V

TRADITION, INSTITUTIONS, PROCESSES, RELIGION

The Hierophant encourages you to look at age-old practices or seek out the advice of a leader before making your own choices. This card does not tell you to seek outdated traditions that don't serve you, but rather to search them out and look at them with a critical eye, gleaning what you can from these timeless sources. There is always a new way to look at things, but the Hierophant is here to remind you that adhering to key principles and rules sometimes has a place as well. It's good to be individualistic, but there is also lots to be learned from tradition—even if that custom comes from a place where you have not felt seen before, like in a church or nuclear family structure. Remember that "tradition" doesn't always mean being stuck in the past or resistant to change, as many have felt in the queer community. Rather, it can encompass just exploring *why* people conform to these rules and what you can take from them. This card can also urge you to join something new, like a gym or class, and prompts you to remember that there is value in learning from others. This card is priming you to learn a lesson from someone or something in the future and is a reminder that conventionality can sometimes have its place in leading you down the right path.

REVERSE: When the Hierophant appears in reverse, it reminds you that you are your own first teacher and guide. Understanding this gives you the ability to challenge the conventions that so often do not benefit those who are marginalized. Now is the time

to move past the confines of the status quo and create your own structures and visions.

THINGS TO CONSIDER: Often, institutions reject queer people, and it's important to trust your intuition about where you feel safe and valued (or not). However, consider what morals or lessons you can take from these experiences. We can only learn so much on our own, and sometimes it's worth it to leave our comfort zones to seek a deeper understanding.

MODELS: Albert Rios — he/him; Alex Luciano — she/her; TK — he/him

The Lovers, VI

LOVE, DESIRE, MAKING CHOICES

The Lovers card has many sides to it, like a beautiful and complicated prism in the sunlight, refracting every color known to the human eye in every direction possible. First and foremost, the Lovers encourage us to follow our hearts, no matter the situation. Only you know deep down what is important to you when it comes to matters of the heart.

This card can represent a very solid relationship, or one that is to come, either romantic or platonic. And that can be the best feeling in the world! If this speaks to you, bask in these loving and desire-filled moments and enjoy every second. The Lovers also can bring to light that a choice must be made in order to advance to the next step in or out of a relationship. Consider your happiness for a moment. Is this the right path for you? Are you fulfilled? Are you settling? What are your true feelings? Dig deep to find these answers within yourself, and even if they are hard to face, they may tell you the next right move on your part. Also consider red flags instead of taking the easy way out and ignoring them.

And remember: queer relationships *aren't* hetero relationships, in the sense that queer relationships are like a next-level experience, with the added elements of an extreme understanding of hardships and evolved ways of thinking about and accepting one another's bodies, identities, desires, and needs. Don't be afraid of what other people think when it comes to whom and how you love.

REVERSE: When the Lovers appear in reverse, it's a signal that you're not in alignment with your heart and true desires. This

might manifest as bad feelings about your relationship with your family, friends, or partner(s). Reflect on your happiness and try to home in on what is causing you this disharmony.

THINGS TO CONSIDER: What is the next step for you and your partner(s)? How do you really feel—what is your heart trying to tell you? If you are in a new relationship, enjoy these beginning and new moments together as they could make it or break it.

MODELS: pau venadito — they/them; Valentine Darling — they/them; Luz Miranda — she/they

The Chariot, VII

WILLPOWER, TRIUMPH, CONFIDENCE

The Chariot is a call to battle and to fight for what you believe is right. Willpower is much needed at this time, as you may be experiencing a bump in the road on your journey. Imagine that your personal chariot is your very own cool customized ride, moving you forward in life and acting as your very own vehicle of expression. You feel confident and strong when you're riding in your chariot, and you can get anything you want when you're cruising in it. When times are tough, as this card suggests, hop on your metaphorical chariot and dive headfirst into the fight with a competitive outlook. Now is the time to seriously battle for what you desire, but keep in mind that if you triumph it is important not to get all cocky over winning—nobody likes a show-off.

REVERSE: Move forward with your goals with focus and determination. Don't fret about the challenges you fear you might face, and use your willpower to provide impetus to make progress. Stay disciplined and consistent and you'll forge a path for yourself.

THINGS TO CONSIDER: What are you fighting for and why is it important to you? Imagine what your own chariot looks like: Does it have fire on the sides? Fluffy seating? A unicorn pulling it? Use imagery to build your confidence while preparing to give it your all in this upcoming battle. Replace aggression with passion.

MODELS: Kreacher — dog; Karli Miller — they/them; Quibbler — dog

Strength, VIII

DETERMINATION, POWER, ENDURANCE

The Strength card calls on you to gather your inner force and determination and to use them to guide you through an obstacle. The Strength card allows you to access the confidence needed to face a scary or intimidating situation head-on. Remind yourself that just as the person on this card is taming a lion, you too can channel your passion and rage into a productive outlet. Let the Strength card remind you that at times your zeal can be overwhelming and needs to be tamed. Access your wild side, but also recognize when it is taking over and controlling you—find the willpower inside of you to accomplish anything. While this card's lion depicts physical strength, it is a reminder to practice accessing your inner strength—your willpower, tenacity, and resilience will take you far.

REVERSE: Do an internal check-in with your sense of self-worth and confidence. The Strength cards calls on you to overcome the parts of yourself that live deep within and are often repressed or neglected. When we are out of tune with these parts of ourselves, they can spill into our lives in a variety of ways.

If you neglect yourself—your *whole* self, not just the parts you show the world—you may end up feeling exhausted, disconnected, and out of touch with your own strength. Spend time building yourself up again!

THINGS TO CONSIDER: What passions are worthy of your time? If you feel stuck, think of a time you felt unable to achieve a lofty goal, and reflect on how you ultimately made it there. Access that inner strength to take you there again. We are much more resilient than we give ourselves credit for.

MODEL: Danny Gee — he/him

The Hermit, IX

SOLITUDE, WISDOM, RETREAT, MEDITATION

The Hermit embodies a quality that society often rejects: solitude. There are many fears behind the idea of being alone, but the Hermit is one card that encourages isolation. This card calls for you to take time for yourself, focusing on deep reflection and alone time. Being alone with yourself can be scary if you don't practice it often, but truly getting to know yourself in silence will only make you stronger, as well as teach you about independence. Remember, you are the only you, and you are the only person who will *always* be there for yourself. There is constantly something new to learn about yourself, whether you are meditating, journaling, or just letting your mind run. Practicing solitude doesn't only mean working on yourself. In some cases, this could be an opportunity to focus your attention on a project or to remove yourself from a negative situation. Learn to be alone but not lonely. Your inner light will guide you!

REVERSE: When the Hermit appears reversed, it might indicate that you're feeling withdrawn from others at this time. It's a good idea to break out of your shell and find ways to step into your community. It's important to have a healthy balance between solitude and togetherness. You're great alone, but sometimes you need others—or maybe they need you. This can also indicate that your inner voice may be weakened—perhaps by listening to somebody else instead of trusting your own intuition. Try to develop a personal relationship with your ego.

THINGS TO CONSIDER: Are you choosing the solitary life or has this fallen into your lap? What area of your life would you like clarity in? Where would you like light shed? Look deep

within. Spend time alone with a journal and let your thoughts flow without holding back. Identify patterns and recurring topics. Learn how to take care of yourself.

MODEL: Heather — she/her

Wheel of Fortune, X

LUCK, CHANGE, DESTINY, FATE

Wheel . . . of . . . Fortune! A stroke of luck! This card may indicate that you've stumbled on, or are about to stumble on, a bit of good luck. However, the wheel is constantly spinning, so this moment may be fleeting. If you're at a low point, let the Wheel of Fortune remind you that everything in life is a cycle and what you are experiencing now will come to an end. If you're at a high point, let it remind you that things will change at some point—but at the same time, remember that these happy moments are something to cherish. This card can also be a reflective pause to think about how you treat others—what goes around comes around, so make sure you're treating others well, even if you disagree with them. This card may remind you that, often, things are outside of your control and you have to roll with the punches. Everything you experience is leading you to your destiny.

REVERSE: The Wheel of Fortune reversed often indicates unexpected change, which may cause stress and resistance. It's likely that this unexpected change is not something you want, but regardless of your desires, it is now your reality. This is a good time to reflect on your relationship to change, power, and control. Reflect on your locus of control in this particular situation and what may have brought you here. This time in contemplation will help you break negative cycles.

THINGS TO CONSIDER: Write a list of things you are in control of and things that are out of your control. Try focusing on what is in your control, rather than the things you cannot change.

MODELS: Tara Shea Burke — she/her;
Muffin FKA Mafia — cat

Justice, XI

JUSTICE, FAIRNESS, LAW

While this card calls to mind legal systems, that is a very narrow interpretation as many legal systems around the world can often be corrupt and unfair, especially to marginalized groups. Let this card remind you that justice as an ideal comes in many shapes and forms. The justice system that this card typically represents—like police, judges, and the courts—doesn't actually demonstrate the breadth and depth of justice. Justice is also social action, working to combat broken systems. Use this card as a reminder of the transformative power of collective action and the morals and values that guide you to seek justice. Hold yourself accountable for your actions—whether they're things in the past you regret or opinions you still hold to be true. Be open to learning from your actions and those of others. This card may appear when you feel at an impasse and need to make a choice—take a step back and try to see all the layers and possible outcomes.

REVERSE: When Justice appears in reverse, it can indicate that you're having an internal conflict that needs reconciliation.

Maybe you're feeling guilty for something you've done, or you're reflecting on a time you weren't true to yourself. Are you being too hard on yourself? Your inner dialogue may be bringing you down—keep in mind that everyone makes mistakes, including you. Forgive yourself. If you've hurt someone else, this is a call to reconcile with them.

THINGS TO CONSIDER: Where are your morals? What is "right"? Think about what values you hold true and how they have changed over time. How can you fight for what is right and come to terms with your wrongdoings? How can you hold others accountable, but better yet, how can you hold yourself accountable?

MODEL: Vico Ortiz — they/him/she (elle/le in Spanish)

The Hanged Man, XII

SACRIFICE, LETTING GO, SURRENDER

If you feel like you've come to an impasse, it's important to pause and change your perspective. The reason you may be feeling stuck is because your old ways of doing things are no longer serving you. It's time to literally turn yourself upside down, to figure out an alternate way to handle this situation. This is not the time to push forward, like you would with the Chariot card, but instead a time to slow down and consider what may be keeping you in this same old routine that isn't bringing you the results you seek.

REVERSE: Surrender to the universe—you can't have control over everything and you've been exhausting yourself by keeping busy through mindless, menial tasks. It's time to pause. Overdoing it carries the risk of burnout, and if you don't slow down and reflect on your choices, behaviors, and mindsets, you are heading straight toward exhaustion. The Hanged Man in reverse can also mean that you are feeling restricted by your circumstances. Maybe a change of perspective is in order. However, if you've already been on a pause, this can be a sign that things are going to start to pick up for you.

THINGS TO CONSIDER: If you can't change your situation, change your attitude toward it. Lie down and look up at the ceiling for a different perspective. Reflect while taking in this different view.

MODEL: Eli Bird — he/him

Death, XIII

TRANSFORMATION, REBIRTH, CLOSURE

Death may seem like a very frightening sight at first, but when you look more closely, it is actually quite an encouraging and necessary card. It represents a part of your life that needs to come to an end, and this will likely happen suddenly or against your will. This can mean the end to a toxic relationship, identity, habit, job, or anything that may be holding you back from your fullest potential and your ultimate truth. It might feel wrong or shocking to you when this door closes, but know that it needs to happen. You don't have to view Death as a negative thing, and in most cases, this card will refer to a "metaphorical death." These things happen in life no matter what, so rather than deny extremely painful times, embrace them and know that they will move you forward to your next step in life. Don't look at Death in the sense of dying, but instead try taking on the perspective that this is your rebirth after the much-needed end to this phase. It is sometimes necessary for us to lose in order to gain.

REVERSE: This card reversed can mean a more wrenching change. You might find yourself feeling resistant to this change because it wasn't part of your plan. As you go through what may be a painful transition, it's important to remember that endings are also new beginnings. Your resistance might be what's holding you back. Instead of looking at unhealthy attachment patterns, you are focusing your energy on what left and on the loss. It's time to accept this change, so that you can begin to move forward.

THINGS TO CONSIDER: What makes you sad about this particular loss? What are you most looking forward to post-rebirth? Now that this door is closed for good, think about the positive things in the future that can come out of this grim situation.

MODELS: Ricky Tyler — he/they; Grace Duong — she/her; Jarred Daniels — he/him

Temperance, XIV

MODERATION, BALANCE, NEUTRALITY

Temperance is a card that's all about finding your center. Representing restraint, moderation, and balance, this card encourages you to identify the excesses in your life and to *take a break* from them. If you've been going through tough times, this card signifies that pain will eventually be alleviated, pushing you to return to regular life, away from all the negativity you've endured. But that rebalancing can only start when you make the decision to relax for a second. Temperance reminds us that sometimes we need to take the neutral path, seeking to understand both sides of a situation and possibly acting as a peacemaker. More literally, Temperance can represent sobriety or a reality check about your behaviors and vices. This card can show you that by analyzing your habits surrounding the potentially harmful things in your life, you can recenter yourself by practicing moderation and restraint.

REVERSE: **You have been overindulging or being excessive in one area of your life, causing an imbalance. This is a sign to commit to more restraint, evenhandedness, and moderation in your**

life. It may be time to examine your life's vision, goals, values, and priorities. If you're not quite feeling like yourself, then pause and do the work to raise your vibration.

THINGS TO CONSIDER: Try meditating or just being still for a few moments. Take in the calm around you and soak in it until some of that peace becomes part of you. When in the middle of a conflict, try imagining the situation from the other person's perspective. Even if it's difficult or sucky, it could give you some clarity. Practice restraint. What does being centered mean to you?

MODEL: matty — they/them

The Devil, XV

NEGATIVITY, ATTACHMENT, RESTRICTION

This card may appear threatening, but it is here to show you that you need to be completely honest with yourself. It's pointing out your true shadow—the forces or ideas that hold you back. What is it that's inhibiting you? The Devil often shows dependency on something, be it another person, a substance, materialism, habits, or your own mind. Often the Devil shows up to remind you that you have control over yourself. You *can* break free of a negative pattern in your life. You must identify it honestly and be real about how it's hindering you. Of course, this isn't an immediate fix—change will take time, and the Devil reminds you to overcome whatever is holding you back step-by-step, giving yourself permission to fail and try again. In order to break free from the pattern that is holding you down, you must accept it as a problem first.

REVERSE: You are breaking free of your bonds! Unhealthy attachments to people, substances, habits, etc., are being released! Or, at the very least, you are in a mental space to see these toxic patterns as an issue and are ready to work on them. It seems you are in a headspace to dig into your repressed and neglected side that may have led to unhealthy patterns. This is a good time to seek out community and/or a therapist for support to help you through this process.

THINGS TO CONSIDER: Is it hard to be honest with yourself when coming to terms with codependency? Why? Write a list of things that may be unhealthy for your personal growth. Trust your gut, even if the truth is scary to confront.

MODELS: Malek Ansari — they/them;
Constance Shumaker — she/her;
Angie Cooper — she/her

The Tower, XVI

CHANGE, REVELATION, AWAKENING

The Tower, with its falling people, is here to remind you that change is on the horizon and unavoidable. Maybe it's the loss of a loved one, a sudden health problem, a failure of some sort, a breakup, or a sudden change of course on your envisioned life path. The Tower often disrupts everything you thought you knew—you had been standing on what you believed was a solid foundation and all of a sudden it's completely uprooted. You might feel like your world is crashing down around you when this change comes or have a moment of clarity in which you realize your world was built on an unstable foundation. This is so confusing and frustrating, as you are forced to suddenly confront all your realities—but remember that you will always get *something* out of this change. That isn't to say that there is inherent good in all changes, but rather that you will learn something moving forward from the disruption. You may need to reassess your life, which can be very uncomfortable, but necessary. The Tower reminds you that there is no avoiding changes, especially those that are totally out of your control, and your job right now is to allow your habitual structure to fall so that you can rebuild it with your new understanding. You will be more resilient and wiser, finding transformation and growth in the destruction.

REVERSE: You are at a place in your life where you are actively questioning your belief systems and values. The reversed Tower is an internal shift in which you are orchestrating the investigation. Take time to strengthen your intuition during this Tower moment as you are relearning who you are.

THINGS TO CONSIDER: Surrender. Be humble to the fact that you cannot control everything—some things are out of your hands and impossible to predict. How can you use your core values to guide you through this change?

MODELS: Luis Miguel Sosa — he/him;
Danny Brito — he/him

The Star, XVII

HOPE, RENEWAL, HAPPINESS

The Star is a beautiful and shining glimmer of hope high in the sky, and right now you are floating up there right beside it. Everything is amazing! You may be feeling inspired and blessed by the universe, connected with yourself and everything around you. That happy-go-lucky feeling you're experiencing is just the beginning. Good health, mental stability, and calming energy are abundant, and your endeavors are successful, putting you in the best mood possible. Allow yourself to dream big and reach for the stars around you at this time. Magic surrounds you and so does the loving embrace of the universe. The Star also brings a sense of renewal to you, stripping away all the unneeded and negative layers from your being and encouraging self-love, self-acceptance, and growth, starting deep down in your core. The transformation from the old you to the new you is happening, and everything is how it needs to be right now. There will always be ups and downs in life, so enjoy these moments while they are in full swing.

REVERSE: You are experiencing really difficult situations, and it seems unfair. As a result you are questioning your faith, and the universe itself, right now. It seems like one bad thing is happening after another. Or you may be feeling overwhelmed and disconnected from what you are doing. It's time to reassess, reflect, and see if there are any lessons for you to learn about yourself here. Are bad things happening or are you taking on too much and dropping the ball? Does it feel like you always end up in negative situations? If so, what patterns are bringing you here? What message does the universe want you to learn from these situations?

THINGS TO CONSIDER: What has been holding you back from being happy up until this moment? What can you get rid of in your life to feel good? What are some practices you can implement in your life to make you feel content and confident with yourself as a person?

MODEL: Riylan M. — she/her

The Moon, XVIII

ILLUSIONS, DECEPTION, FEAR

The Moon has a dark and deep energy that is a powerful, reversed version of the Sun's. Its eerie yet magical beams subtly edge their way through the dark of night as they light your path, but there are fears and doubts inside of you that are holding you in place. Although deception and illusions are present with the Moon, you must hold fast and remember that you are *in control.* You may be afraid of what's coming next, but don't let that uncertainty take over your life. Take this card as a call to look your fears in the face. Get to know them—conquer them, even. If you are feeling anxious or weary about a situation, don't make any sudden moves—the Moon signifies unstable and amplified emotions, which can sometimes interfere with making the right decision. Sit with this uncertainty and wait. Get to know yourself, the root of your fears, and confront them. By the time you are finished, you should have more information about the situation at hand, and you will be able to move forward in your intended direction. This card does not have to be a negative card. The Moon encourages healing, but to do so you must face whatever is weighing you down and keeping you from being your best self. And remember, your intuition can be your handiest tool when deception is afoot.

REVERSE: You've spent some time worrying and feeling anxious, and those negative energies are finally receding—you feel like you can at last realize the impact these negative thoughts are having on your life. This is liberating for you. However, recognize that while illusion, anxiety, and fear can be limiting and hold you in place, they are still emotions that deserve to be dealt with. This can be a warning that you've begun to push any negative feelings inside, which will just cause them to resurface later. Listen to your inner voice and trust that you already have all the tools and answers you need within you.

THINGS TO CONSIDER: Freewrite anything that is on your mind right now, and don't hold back. What did you uncover? Destroy the paper afterward if needed. Single out a fear of yours and say it out loud—imagine it leaving the small chamber of your brain and entering the vast and infinite universe, where it can get lost.

MODELS: Pepper — dog; Cassio — dog

The Sun, XIX

POSITIVITY, WARMTH, RADIANCE, ABUNDANCE

The Sun symbolizes good times, good health, and good moods all around. It brings the kind of warmth and joy into your life that feels just plain wonderful, giving you the positive and beautiful energy to get through the rough stuff. It illuminates you when you are feeling down or doubtful and takes away all that fear surrounding you. It also signifies a boost in health and vitality. This card brings radiance and happiness whenever it shows up and will brighten the mood of all the cards it is pulled with. We all need a little bit more sunshine in our lives, so don't take this special card for granted!

REVERSE: The Sun reversed is a call to embrace your inner child and let it out! You've been caught up in "adulting" and the stress that comes with it, and it's time to let yourself experience true joy. This can be a sign that you've been so involved in the hustle and grind of life that you're letting these sunny moments slip you by. Maybe you've just experienced some serious setbacks that you're struggling to recover from—the Sun is here to remind you that these obstacles are only temporary.

THINGS TO CONSIDER: **What are some things that you are grateful for in this moment? What makes you the happiest? How can you share this positivity with the people around you? Remember this feeling and save it for a time when you need it the most.**

Judgment, XX

HUMILITY, ACCEPTANCE, REBIRTH

The Judgment card calls on you to seek *your* truth. Maybe it's time to call yourself out. How are you treating yourself and others? This card may bring to mind the notion of karma—or what goes around comes around—so think about how you are manifesting a better world. This card reminds you that not only are you able to change your life, but you *must* take a deeper look every now and then to adjust yourself. Maybe you have had a change of heart or a new desire—if that is the case, and Judgment is present, it means that you should accept this feeling and shed the fears that come with something new. It's okay to be judged, by yourself even, because it can bring you to a new realization and allow you to change for the better. Learn from your mistakes, evaluate your past experiences, and move forward. Let go and reflect on the past, but not with regret—this is simply a time to continue on. Maybe it's the moment to accept an apology from a friend, move past a grudge, forgive yourself for past mistakes, and so on.

REVERSE: **You are spending some quality time reflecting on yourself, which is allowing you to gain an understanding of the themes that run through your life. You're gaining greater knowledge of how to avoid similar negative situations in the future, and reconciling with past events and mistakes. Judgment calls upon you to forgive yourself for past regressions—all you can do is move forward. In this moment, trust that the universe has your back, and push through to your greater calling. Playing it safe will only get you so far.**

THINGS TO CONSIDER: **Take inventory of the heavy feelings you've been holding on to. How can you right those wrongs? Did someone else wrong you? How can you move past that—forgiveness, acknowledgment, considering their perspective, a conversation, cutting them out? Think about the pros and cons of taking a next step, considering how you want to change your life for the better.**

MODELS: Edrian Pangilinan — he/him;
Lee Ellen Fanning — she/her;
Melody Lee Rosa — she/her; Alex Teschel — she/they;
Meg Thompson — she/her;
Sofia Kon. — she/they

The World, XXI

WHOLENESS, ACHIEVEMENT, COMPLETION

The World signifies completion and wholeness, the end of the journey. The cycle is finally complete, and everything you have been working for is coming full circle. Accept congratulations humbly and take a moment to be proud of your accomplishments. This card can also be an affirmation of your identity, as it suggests that you are making your way into the next steps of living your best queer life. But since this is an end-of-the-journey card, you should also consider taking a break or a vacation. Enjoy the progress you've made thus far and make some time for yourself now.

REVERSE: Closure, closure, closure. Finding closure is a step toward healing and may require you to do some intense thinking—journaling, meditation, and therapy are all good ways to allow yourself to move on. You may be thinking about starting a new journey or jumping into a big project, but are afraid to start. Remember that the bottom is only temporary, and your patience and perseverance will pay off if you're truly in search of your higher journey. Feel confident setting lofty goals, since you know that you have all the tools to reach them, despite however many setbacks and restarts it may take.

THINGS TO CONSIDER: Reflect on your accomplishment(s) and consider the journey it took for you to achieve it (them). Do you feel whole? What important things have you learned along the way? Take the wisdom and strength you've gained and never let them go.

MODEL: Miranda — she/her

Ace of Wands
II
III
IV
V
VI
VII
VIII
IX

Wands

Ace of Wands

BIRTH, BEGINNINGS, INSPIRATION

This card is the first of the Minor Arcana and symbolizes a new journey. Lead with your heart and start exploring your big ideas—inspiration and optimism are plentiful with the Ace of Wands, so take an idea and run with it! You may be feeling inspired and full of goals, or perhaps you are ready to approach a situation with a brand-new outlook. Consider this card permission to do what your heart desires and a reminder to be on the lookout for opportunities that align with your true purpose.

REVERSE: You may be feeling like you are stuck, with a low drive to accomplish things or as if you don't know what your passions are. You might be reconsidering your life's work.

THINGS TO CONSIDER: Have you felt a calling to begin something recently? Where has that message been coming from? Keep an open mind about your long-term plan—this will help make any roadblocks along the way less hurtful. Imagine your ultimate goal and work toward it a little every day. Are you following your passions? Do you know where your heart lies? Use this as an opportunity to reconsider your priorities.

Two of Wands

FUTURE PLANNING, PROGRESS, DIRECTION

It's time to take action steps to continue manifesting your great plans! The Two of Wands encourages you to focus, continue on your path, see the big picture, and think about the long term. You're likely on the right path already, but it's time to decide *where* your ideas are leading you. Now is not the time to stop and take a breather! Working hard is essential to bring your goals to fruition. Remember, great things come from small beginnings. Just an idea or a first step can lead you to greatness. If you are in a partnership of any kind, whether for business or love, move forward together, not separately. Use this energy to support your dreams, whether emotional or professional.

REVERSE: **You might feel like you don't know where to start when planning or executing your goals. This is a good time to journal and think about *what* your goals are, get clear on your values, and develop steps to move forward.**

THINGS TO CONSIDER: **Set small goals leading up to your bigger goal so you can tangibly mark your progress, especially if you are feeling like the road is taking so long to travel. Keep**

your priorities in mind when you feel yourself straying from your path.

MODEL: Elsa G. aka Wild Black — she/they

Three of Wands

PROGRESS, EXPANSION, ENVISIONING THE FUTURE

Yippee! The Three of Wands is a card of good fortune, whether in relationships, your career, or your dreams. You're in the sweet spot for moving forward with future plans and right where you need to be. When this card appears in your reading, you should take a moment to reflect on how you got to where you are now in order to look forward and decide how to progress. Perhaps use this time to consider any upcoming obstacles that may lie ahead—this gives you time to prepare. This card encourages the broadening of your horizons, as well as self-exploration to promote development in your creative journey. Remember that communication can play an important role when executing plans, so don't let that slip away in your excitement.

REVERSE: You're stuck in your comfort zone, which leaves you limited! You may end up frustrated when you cannot achieve your goals because of your fear of taking risks.

THINGS TO CONSIDER: How can you continue to keep things running smoothly? Which practices are working for you and which are not? How comfortable are you in taking the next step? Communicate with others who could be affected by your plans and ideas.

MODEL: Oran Colwell — he/him

Four of Wands

CELEBRATION, COMPLETION

Woo-hoo! Party!!! The Four of Wands signifies that something has been completed or a special milestone has been hit. It's a card of celebration, which is why there are so many exclamation points in this description! Take a moment to acknowledge yourself and feel good about your accomplishments! If you feel like you don't have a real reason to celebrate, just relish the fact that you are here in this moment, reflecting and working on yourself. You're probably doing better than you think, if not from your perspective, then perhaps from someone else's. Take the time to just sit back and celebrate where you are! If you don't like to celebrate yourself, celebrate those around you whom you appreciate!

REVERSE: **Maybe you aren't quite ready for the celebration that this card usually calls for, but you are on the road to achieving your goals. It's okay to be proud of the steps you are taking to get there, even if they seem small so far or your progress feels stagnant.**

THINGS TO CONSIDER: **When was the last time you took time to celebrate yourself? What is your ideal day to acknowledge yourself and the progress you've made? Take time to celebrate something today, even if it's the smallest thing.**

MODELS: Nic Charlie Perez — she/her;
Rachel Brown — she/her

Five of Wands

CHALLENGING TIMES, COMPETITION, CONFLICT, TENSION, CHAOS

The Five of Wands may show up when you've got the impression that everything is scattered and out of reach. You might feel a sense of conflict, but know with conflict comes transformation. Conflict is natural and necessary for growth—nobody's path is always easy. When this card appears, think about how to maintain a sense of control and clarity through this conflict. Don't let things get under your skin, and don't let pain or hard feelings cloud your thinking—keep a cool head and find peace within, even if it means compromising on something you are reluctant to lose complete control over. Removing yourself from a situation, even temporarily, may give you the space to find peace and lead you to shine a light on what you couldn't see before in the midst of the chaos.

REVERSE: You may be feeling inner turmoil rather than a sense of conflict with others. Spend some time getting to know the parts of yourself that are out of alignment, focusing on the head and the heart.

THINGS TO CONSIDER: **Ground yourself. Find calm in calamity. Get down to the root of it: What is bothering you and putting you on edge? What does the tension you are feeling stem from? Practice imagining yourself in someone else's shoes. What does that perspective look like? We all have truths, even if some people's truths may be different from and in conflict with our own.**

MODELS: Leo — they/them; Nina Alexander — she/her; Jini Valence — she/they; Bailey Sell — he/him; Kevin August — he/him

Six of Wands

AMBITIONS, SUCCESS, VICTORY

Whew, your hard work has paid off! The Six of Wands represents success. You powered through distractions and focused on the task at hand despite obstacles thrown your way. When this card appears, take a minute to pat yourself on the back for your accomplishments—others have noticed your perseverance and resourcefulness! No need to be modest right now. Savor the positive reactions that come from your accomplishments. This kind of attention has the potential to give you even more strength and power to push you to continue forward toward the bigger picture.

REVERSE: You might be feeling stuck, relying on others to validate your success and hard work. Your confidence may be at a low point, but take the time to give yourself some self-loving and validation.

THINGS TO CONSIDER: Use this time to reflect on the struggles you've overcome to get to this point. If your fears of moving forward are creeping up in the back of your mind, think about where those fears are coming from. Consider whether you are in it for the right reasons. Take all the praise and positivity and channel that into your future endeavors—but remember to keep a humble outlook on your accomplishments.

MODELS: Chess Needham — he/him;
Ash Molesso — she/her; Cassie Carrasco — she/they

Seven of Wands

SELF-CONFIDENCE, COURAGE, BOUNDARIES

Your success hasn't gone unnoticed, which means that you may have caught the attention of haters. Negative and critical feedback can be annoying, but it is a reminder to stand your ground when your values, beliefs, and boundaries are challenged. Don't respond impulsively. Instead, be prepared and expect this kind of backlash from others. Lead with your courage and passion. Put your inner strength front and center and stay cool, calm, and collected. Don't let others dampen your success.

REVERSE: You may be feeling self-doubt as a result of listening to what others say instead of what you know to be true. Insecurity is a terrible feeling that overcomes us all every now and then, but you can stand up to that voice in your head—or the actual voices of people critiquing you—and say no! You may be feeling full of passionate rage, but know when and where to let it show. Everyone is entitled to their beliefs, but that doesn't mean you can't fight for what you think is right. Just choose your battles wisely.

THINGS TO CONSIDER: Think about a figure in your life who is the epitome of confidence—channel their energy, pushing all your doubts and insecurities aside. How does it feel to be on top and without worry? Write down all your doubts and then toss them in the trash. You can stand your ground and also be open to learning at the same time.

MODEL: Imani Russell — they/them

Eight of Wands

SWIFTNESS, SUDDEN CHANGE, ALIGNMENT

The Eight of Wands suggests moving toward alignment. Sudden change may come as a reminder that obstacles and opportunities can happen at any moment, throwing your plans off course. When this card appears in your reading, go with the flow and be open to changes in your plans, even if you thought they were fixed and concrete. This card suggests that with these swift changes, opportunities arise that may require you to act fast. Go with it!

REVERSE: You may feel resistant to change, or there may be a delay holding back your plans. This is a great time to step back and slow down, reassess, and look at any challenges in a new light.

THINGS TO CONSIDER: Can you use this change or opportunity to your benefit? Does it align with your end goals or beliefs? If you can't shift your circumstances, can you try altering the way you think about or deal with them?

Nine of Wands

RESILIENCE, STRENGTH, PERSEVERANCE

You're almost there, and your resilience is shining through! You're in the final stretch, so whatever you do, don't give up now. When you're feeling fearful, unsuccessful, are experiencing a setback, or things just start to seem so difficult, do what it takes to push through and finish. All of the Wand cards that come before the Nine of Wands are your support system, so remember to look for them when you're feeling like you can't make it across the finish line.

You are safe and your perseverance will help get you past whatever last-minute obstacles or cold feet you are experiencing on this particular journey. Really look at all you've built for yourself—whether that's a physical manifestation, a project, or just your own inner strength and mental fortitude. Don't let anything tear you down, you've worked so hard for this.

REVERSE: You're near the end, but feeling so overwhelmed at all the obstacles that have been thrust onto your path. You may be feeling guarded and defensive or afraid to ask for help. Now is a good time to strengthen your intuition and focus on finding your inner strength and courage.

THINGS TO CONSIDER: Imagine the finish line. If you are feeling self-doubt right now, think about where it stems from. Remember a time you accomplished something. Write a list of all the things you did in order to get you this far in your journey and reflect on all the hard work you've done.

MODEL: Rico Castillo — they/them

Ten of Wands

BURDENS, RESPONSIBILITY, COMPLETION

Action, action, action. The Ten of Wands represents blockages and burdens that might be holding you back. Realize that this extra weight, although heavy, is only temporary. Think about whether you can make this current problem more manageable by shedding baggage, getting rid of unnecessary responsibilities or tasks, or relinquishing some of your control by delegating to others. Try to lift some weight off your shoulders—this card reminds you that you are near the end of this difficult cycle, so try to focus on the light at the end of the tunnel.

REVERSE: You may be doing too much on your own and struggling to let go of control. Remember to focus on what you are here to do, and keep in mind that putting too much on yourself will not help you in the long run. You don't want to burn out so close to the finish line.

THINGS TO CONSIDER: Try saying no. Write a list of things that you feel are holding you down and why. Use this list to reassess what is necessary and what can be dropped. Shed a responsibility—ask for help if you need a break.

MODEL: Maxx Rayne — she/her

Page of Wands

FREE SPIRIT, DISCOVERY, INSPIRATION

You're ready to embark on a new creative journey and embrace it with enthusiasm! Don't let the fact that you don't know exactly where you're headed hold you back or make you doubt yourself. This card has a restless energy—you have countless ideas you want to work on, but you may benefit from taking time to map out your strategy and figure out which ideas align with your big picture goals. Share your ideas with a friend; sometimes speaking a dream into existence is enough to get it off the ground.

REVERSE: Your idea isn't fleshed out, and you've tried many things with little success. The Page of Wands is reminding you to be adaptable and that failing is part of learning something new or getting better at something. Although you want to achieve greatness, remember that you often must start from the bottom and be ready to adjust and try again when you fail.

THINGS TO CONSIDER: Be a yes person! Say yes to something you didn't think you normally would—go with your friend to their weird class or swing on a swing at the playground. Embrace the unknown. Write down all your wild and exciting ideas and look back at them when you feel uninspired or bored.

MODEL: Natasha R. Johnson — she/her/unicorn

Knight of Wands

INTENSITY, BRILLIANCE, FIRE

You are ready to dive into a new endeavor in your life, be it a creative project, career, love, or anything else. The Knight of Wands symbolizes intensity and speed, meaning that amazing ideas can swiftly change your path. The Knight knows how to harness their fire within! It's time to use this energy to keep going and push through. You have the unique ability to take your idea, manifest it, and turn it into something. Others may perceive you as confident and charismatic, which helps to fuel your passions. This confidence moves you to act without fear of failure.

REVERSE: This energy, when unhinged, can lead to impulsivity and poor planning. This might make you feel as if you don't know where to direct your energy. Slow down and get in touch with your intuition. If you are lacking the spark the Knight of Wands brings, it might be time to explore something new to fuel your passions.

THINGS TO CONSIDER: Try channeling the Knight of Wands' energy into your own life if you are feeling stuck at the beginning of something new. Write a list of what might be preventing you from seeing what is keeping you where you are. If you identify with the Knight of Wands, don't let your pride and ego get in the way when it comes to collaboration.

MODEL: Toni Rowe — she/her

Queen of Wands

CONFIDENCE, ENCOURAGEMENT, COURAGE, DETERMINATION

You're confident, optimistic, and simply ooze good vibes. A natural social butterfly, your presence is a delight to be around. When this card appears in your reading, it signals that you are confident and comfortable in your own skin and ready to express yourself fully to the rest of the world. When you exist as your most authentic self, you give permission and courage to others to live up to their fullest potential too. Your presence reminds others that they are powerful. A Queen of Wands might signify a ride-or-die friend who uplifts you and cares as much about your success as their own. If *you* are the Queen of Wands, then relish the fact that you are such a helper—you give others this feeling of security that allows them to go after their goals. You truly want everyone to succeed and care about the community.

REVERSE: The Queen of Wands shows you your shadow, the parts of yourself that are inextricably you but you don't like to show. You may neglect, ignore, or simply dislike these parts of

yourself. Maybe you are afraid to expose them for fear of what the community might think. The Queen of Wands is a reminder to embrace this side of you—it *is* you, after all—in order to be your full self. This will give you a better understanding of your values, convictions, or belief systems. This hidden part of you may manifest as a wallflower rather than a social butterfly, but don't let that make you feel weak. It's not always the loudest or most confident person who has it all together.

THINGS TO CONSIDER: What can you do with this confidence to help inspire and uplift others? Say yes to a new opportunity that seems daunting. Remember that the Queen of Wands' confidence lives deep within, so don't let naysayers get you down.

MODELS: Riley M. — she/her; Cannoli — cat

King of Wands

LEADER, VISIONARY, INTENTIONAL

The King of Wands, in their visionary nature, draws others in as they see the bigger picture. They have all the ideas and charisma, but choose to delegate tasks in order to involve the community in reaching a goal. When this card appears in your reading, you are manifesting your goals through the support of those around you. Others rely on you to be mature, charismatic, and intentional. The King of Wands is not afraid to ask for help—they may hold all the revolutionary ideas but know that they can't do it on their own.

REVERSE: You may feel uncomfortable or undeserving in a position of power, or you're about to embark on a project that is too large to go at solo. Now is a good time to work on your self-advocacy skills. You have all the power you need to take on a new challenge. If others seem to see you as arrogant, this may be an indication to check your ego.

THINGS TO CONSIDER: Now may be a great time to write a goal book with all of the ideas and dreams that come to you—you never know when they might come in handy.

MODEL: Vincent O. Webb — he/him

Ace of Cups

II

III

IV

V

VI

VII

VIII

IX

Cups

Ace of Cups

NEW LOVE, EMOTIONAL FULFILLMENT, COMPASSION, INTUITION

At the start of something new and wonderful, you're overflowing with love, joy, and expressiveness! The Ace of Cups signifies this new beginning, and your creativity and compassion are amplified beyond compare at this time. You are basically the heart eyes emoji right now. Bask in it! Soak it up! When this card shows up in your reading, you'll have the opportunity to experience emotional fulfillment, spiritual connection, and a release of burdens. This could be in the form of a new friendship, work connection, or partnership of some sort. You may cross paths with a new person who suddenly becomes part of your chosen family. This card is a sign to say *YES*—yes to love, yes to new connections, and yes to the positive energy you feel coming your way.

REVERSE: You may be feeling more closed off than usual, repressing your emotions and feelings. Now is a good time to get in tune with yourself—think self-love and pour your positivity inward.

THINGS TO CONSIDER: How can you take this new beginning and cultivate it into a long-lasting and ever-growing thing? Be open to new opportunities and friendships.

Two of Cups

CONNECTION, LUST-LOVE, BLISS, SYNERGY

The Two of Cups represents a human connection so strong that it is blissful; everything is balanced and perfectly in place. This isn't exclusive to romantic connections—it can happen with anyone in your life. The Two of Cups is a sign that you're right where you need to be and with whomever you are supposed to be. Cooperation, respect, and a deep understanding of one another and the flow of your love will make you feel like you're on top of the world. You're on the same page with this human—they're benefiting from you in the same way you are vibing with them. If you've been experiencing a rocky time, harmony will soon emerge. Remember to nurture this loving bond, as you must communicate and grow together, rather than apart.

REVERSE: You may be feeling out of alignment with your soul purpose or just out of sync. You should prioritize having this intimate relationship with yourself and focus on inner love and care.

THINGS TO CONSIDER: Take time to communicate your feelings to your partner(s), friend, family member, or literally any person, whatever relation they may have to you. Write them a love letter, telling them all the ways they bring joy into your life. Remember this feeling.

MODELS: Anays Torres — she/her;
Ziggy — cat; Kathryn Frances — they/she

Three of Cups

FRIENDSHIP, CREATIVITY, COLLABORATION, SUPPORT

The Three of Cups reminds you to celebrate and be in the company of friends and loved ones. It comes up in a time of abundance, when you are supported and loved by those closest to you. It serves as a reminder to enjoy the time spent with your friends, family, chosen family, and favorite people. This card also suggests creative collaboration and signifies a time to band together artistically with those you connect with.

REVERSE: **You need to prioritize alone time when this card appears in the reverse. Think about your self-care routine and how you help yourself when you feel completely depleted. Repair and rejuvenate!**

THINGS TO CONSIDER: **Have a party with your closest friends. Communicate to the people in your life how much they mean to you, even if it seems out of the blue. Acknowledge your support system in life and thank the people who are part of it.**

MODELS: KNLH — she/her;
Kaiba Linthicum — he/they; Tenaya Jo — they/them

Four of Cups

DISCONTENT, BOREDOM, APATHY

The Four of Cups can creep into your life when you begin to find your situation undesirable and are spending energy reevaluating it and going within. You may feel bored or tired of the monotony of the day-to-day—or like the grass is greener on the other side—but not quite ready to take that leap into something else. While the Four of Cups predicts this uncomfortable feeling, it ultimately encourages you to reframe the way you perceive things. Reflect on your current situation and try to see it from a different angle. See if you can be grateful rather than upset, and remember that sometimes you can't change a situation. If that is the case here, then all you can control is how you think about or deal with it. If you find yourself looking for change or yearning for what you can't have, do something about it instead of just sitting and wishing—whether that means going out and getting what you want or coming to terms with what is obtainable for you at this time.

REVERSE: You feel drawn to retreat and go within. You may be feeling disheartened and not ready to deal with it all. You prefer to spend time alone, but remember, community is important too. Honor your alone time and friendships!

THINGS TO CONSIDER: Open up your mind: Why are you unhappy? Lots of things are out of our control, but that doesn't mean we should dwell too much on the things that upset us. Say aloud a list of positive things in your life right now.

MODEL: Ko S. — he/they

Five of Cups

LOSS, DISTRESS, GRIEF, DISAPPOINTMENT

The Five of Cups indicates hardship or loss. You may be dealing with grief in the form of a broken heart, a lost relationship, or you may just be in complete distress. Don't get too tangled up in these disappointing feelings and wallow in them. When the time is right, you will be able to look past your loss and see that there is more waiting for you on the other side. Sometimes looking in another direction is all you need to see what opportunities lie ahead. The negative may be your focus right now, but the Five of Cups is here to remind you that once the clouds clear and your tears dry, not *all* is lost.

REVERSE: You feel disappointed and are blaming yourself for what happened. Lean into self-forgiveness and remember—you cannot undo the past or change it; you did the best you could at the time.

THINGS TO CONSIDER: **Consider the other party's situation and perhaps reevaluate your expectations of other people. Take your time. There is no need to rush your feelings, especially because the only way out is through.**

MODEL: Mai Ireland — they/them

Six of Cups

INNOCENCE, NOSTALGIA, MEMORIES

The Six of Cups draws us back to those magical, simpler moments when everything felt wonderful and there seemed to be no worries in the world. This card recalls happy memories, joyful times, and the naivete we had before we worried about taxes and rent and coming out and all that terrifying real-life stuff. Now is a good time to connect with those good memories, and even the folx who are in them with you. This card acts as a reminder that you can and should look to your past for answers, especially when dealing with a situation that brings up memories. Looking back and reflecting can offer insights, no matter the situation. The Six of Cups can also be a gentle reminder that it's okay to take a step back from your hard work and play like your inner child wants to, even if just for a bit. Run around outside, pick flowers, play card games with your friends. These activities can be healing when you're feeling lost and overwhelmed in the throes of adulthood.

REVERSE: You're focusing on the past, which is making it tough to live in the present. This is a good time to move on from your history and stop feeling imprisoned by it. Focus on acceptance of the past, because you cannot change it. Get in touch with your inner child and create a safe space for yourself.

THINGS TO CONSIDER: Go back to your roots. Reflect. How have you dealt with specific situations in the past versus how you would deal with them now? Is something coming up from your past that you are having difficulties dealing with? Do something that awakens the childlike part of your soul.

Seven of Cups

ILLUSION, OPPORTUNITIES, CHOICES

The Seven of Cups is a card of forward movement through new opportunities, though be warned: some of these openings may be illusions carrying deceit. When there are so many options, it can be difficult to choose the right one for you. You may want to go for the nice and easy choice, or the most exciting one, but in times like these you should really listen to your gut. Try your best to weigh all options based on whether they align with your goals and beliefs. Evaluation of each option is key—what kind of work goes into each choice and what benefits will you reap? This card can also suggest wishful thinking about what you want for yourself in the future. However, thinking is just that. Nothing will happen unless you start making moves! Contemplating a goal and working toward a goal are two very different forms of action, and now is the time to take that step forward. Try choosing one objective to focus on, rather than attempting to make all your goals happen at once. Spend time with each idea and figure out which ones are the most attainable. Start from there, achieving tiny victories for yourself, and then move on to the bigger and more time-consuming ideas. Do what feels right for you.

REVERSE: You may be feeling overwhelmed by all the choices in front of you. Listen to your intuition, reflect on each choice, and then act with purpose.

THINGS TO CONSIDER: Is something holding you back from moving forward with a plan or an idea? Are your goals realistic and achievable? Weigh your options. Start somewhere small.

MODEL: Tara Suess — she/her

Eight of Cups

STAGNATION, MOVING ON, LETTING GO

The Eight of Cups is a high-priority action card, encouraging us to drop the negativity from our lives and move on. This card appears when it seems like there is nothing left for you. You may be feeling like you've put your all into jobs, people, and behaviors, only to find that your efforts are not reciprocated. Now is the time to ditch what doesn't sustain you and move forward into something that does contribute to your higher purpose. Think of it as saying goodbye to the things that are holding you back and hello to bigger and better things that serve you. Discover yourself and what you desire—if you don't walk away from the past, you won't be able to make room for a richer and more fulfilling life.

REVERSE: **You know deep down that it's imperative to walk away, but you're having trouble making this choice, maybe out of fear of the unknown or fear of disappointment or maybe because you've found comfort in familiarity. This is a good time to think about what's best for you in the long run, not just what's comfortable in the moment.**

THINGS TO CONSIDER: **Imagine a door closing and another one opening. What do you see in the new doorway? Seek outside help from a group or friend if you are having trouble walking away. Do an activity that you love—something for yourself that you enjoy.**

MODEL: V. Arias — she/her

Nine of Cups

HAPPINESS, CELEBRATION, GRATITUDE

The Nine of Cups is a card of joy, joy, joy! This is a card of manifestations and wishes—the stars have aligned just for you and you are experiencing harmony at last! This card is known as the "wish" card—maybe this means your wish has come true or that it may soon. Use this energy to dream big and celebrate. Be grateful for everything in your life right now and bask in this happiness.

REVERSE: You may feel discontent or out of touch with what you value. Reevaluate and reflect on what is important to you.

THINGS TO CONSIDER: What does it feel like to have your dreams come true? Remember this feeling and save it for a time you are feeling down. Write a list of things you are grateful for and choose one to celebrate.

MODEL: Christien Seth Wills — they/them

Ten of Cups

FULFILLMENT, CONTENTEDNESS, COMPLETION, HOME

The Ten of Cups signifies the light at the end of the tunnel, the best outcome, and an end to the journey you've been on for quite some time. It's a happy, harmonious card that brings joy and fulfillment your way, leaving you feeling complete and pleased. Good moods abound when this card appears in your reading! You have clarity and can see and appreciate the people who helped you along the way, and now is a wonderful time to bask in one another's company. This gives you the power to push distractions aside and home in on your true gratitude for people in your life.

REVERSE: You are looking for clarity on exactly what happiness means to you—you feel disengaged from and disharmonious with your loved ones. Now is a good time to try to envision what harmony looks like to you.

THINGS TO CONSIDER: Write a list of the actions people in your life have done for you for which you are grateful. Remember this feeling of happiness toward your friends and/or family.

MODELS: Brandon Connolly — he/him; Mikayla Seaman Connolly — she/her

Page of Cups

OPEN, DREAMY, YOUNG AT HEART

The Page of Cups is here to show you a new opportunity or path that you haven't considered before. They encourage you to open your mind to any and all things—you might discover something completely unexpected, even if it seems out of reach! This card may be showing itself to you in the form of a dream, a spontaneous connection with a stranger, or a brand-new opportunity to try something you haven't before. The Page of Cups can represent falling in love—be that with yourself, who you are becoming, someone new, or even a new or rediscovered interest or idea. Embrace this dreamy feeling and explore it! You might receive something unexpected, and this card is encouraging you to embrace it with open arms. You may be a bit naive at this moment, but what's important is that you go with the flow, trusting your intuition and open mind.

REVERSE: You might be feeling overcritical of yourself, or blocked in your creativity. Focus on your intuition.

THINGS TO CONSIDER: Write down your dreams and desires. Now fold up that piece of paper you wrote on until it can't fold anymore and consider the fact that achieving your dreams might happen in ways you might never expect.

MODEL: Ricardo Agraso — he/they

Knight of Cups

CHARMING, CREATIVE, EMPATHETIC

The Knight of Cups represents someone who is in touch with their feelings and emotions and is friendly and charming. They often use their emotional intuition to connect deeply with people. Their charm means that they are often flirty and romantic heartbreakers—the Knight of Cups is known for intensity over longevity! They might already know what they want or may be searching for something to spark their flame. Whatever the case, the Knight of Cups encourages you to harness this energy and channel it into your journey, whether by experimenting with your identity or working toward longer-term goals.

REVERSE: You may be feeling stuck in the brainstorming stage of a creative process.

THINGS TO CONSIDER: Take some time between jobs, lovers, or activities for yourself. Practice some alone time because you are just as important as everyone else, and you need your love too! Ask yourself what is more important to you: longevity or intensity? It's up to you to decide what you do and don't like.

MODEL: Skylar Riley — they/them

Queen of Cups

SPIRITUAL, INTUITIVE, COMPASSIONATE, CONNECTED

The Queen of Cups is empathetic, soulful, and sympathetic. The Queen of Cups represents someone who embodies a nurturing role—they listen to others and truly care. They keep their friends close and guard them as the matriarch of their chosen family. The Queen is able to tune in and understand what others are going through, allowing them to feel seen and heard. They may be a healer, coach, friend, or mediator. This card encourages you to go with the flow while trusting your intuition and heart. The Queen is strong and able to get through hard times by staying true to themself and trusting their gut.

REVERSE: Your own emotional well-being is the priority right now. Check in and ask a couple of questions: Are you feeling overwhelmed or out of touch with your own feelings? Are you taking on the feelings of others and sitting in codependent relationships? Remember to tune in to your needs before anyone else's.

THINGS TO CONSIDER: Meditate. Seek out those who need your help or seek help from *your* personal Queen of Cups.

MODEL: Zoe Davis — she/her

King of Cups

OPEN-MINDED, BALANCE, EMPATHETIC

The King of Cups is balanced, even, and has a high capacity for emotional intelligence. This person is usually caring, loving, and knows that being gentle and soft is not a form of weakness—they can fully accept their feelings without fear of judgment or shame. The King of Cups favors serving their community rather than ruling over it, making activism a huge passion. This card may be a call to surround yourself with positive people if you're lacking those in your life. Creative and caring by nature, you use your authority and power for the good of others. Remember that being in touch with your emotions is hot, and we could all use a little more positivity and encouragement when talking about our feelings.

REVERSE: You may be feeling extra vulnerable and easily bothered or moody. You're exploring your triggers and your subconscious mind. Remember that being vulnerable is not a weakness.

THINGS TO CONSIDER: What does this card mean to you? Break down the teachings society has instilled in your brain on how to show or hide emotions. Redefine emotional stability for yourself in a way that encourages actually *feeling*!

MODEL: maya finoh — they/them

Ace of Swords

II

III

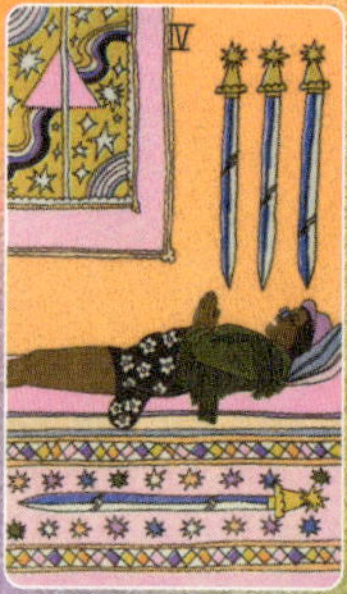
IV

V

VI

VII

VIII

IX

Page of Swords

Swords

Knight of Swords

Queen of Swords

King of Swords

Ace of Swords

NEW BEGINNINGS, CLARITY, TRUTH

The Ace of Swords signifies a new journey that may have begun with a loss. It's bittersweet insofar as it is a reminder that sometimes you have to lose something to gain something, whether that's a relationship, a physical object, or emotional baggage. This loss will give you that aha moment in which you gain mental clarity and a shift in perspective, allowing you to begin this new phase. You now have a fresh outlook that brings clarity or truth to a certain situation. This card literally sheds light on the negativity in your life and asks you to find the determination and willpower to cut it away. Remember, nothing comes without a cost, so be aware that you may have to make sacrifices, but they will be worth it to move forward.

REVERSE: **You may be experiencing a breakthrough, shedding old ways of understanding and communicating. If you feel bogged down by a certain situation, spend time thinking about it in order to gain more mental clarity.**

THINGS TO CONSIDER: **Imagine all the things in your life hanging from a tree like fruit. Which would be the first one you**

would cut away? Try making a pro and con list about your situation. Study it. Writing your thoughts and feelings down on paper helps with making decisions. Do right by what you believe in.

Two of Swords

STALEMATE, BLOCKED PATH, IMPASSE

The Two of Swords represents a roadblock or stalemate, possibly with regard to a difficult decision. You are blinded and unsure of which path to take or where to go next, or maybe you know what you want, but your vision on how to get there is unclear. The energy of this card reminds you that when you want a black-and-white solution to a gray issue it is just not possible. This card calls upon you to meditate and think with nuance, rather than jump into action. Try taking your heart out of the situation for this one and use logic to determine your path to move forward. This card may also come up when you're avoiding making a decision because you're fearful of the repercussions, but remember that not making a choice is a decision too.

REVERSE: You may be feeling overwhelmed and completely stuck, unable to move forward at all. It's a good idea to step back and look at the situation by journaling, listening to yourself with honesty, and even talking it out with others.

THINGS TO CONSIDER: What is holding you back? Consider all sides of your situation. Try altering your expectations or figuring out a compromise to move forward. Dig deep for the truth and face it, because even if it hurts now, it has the potential to give you strength and turn you into the person you are meant to be.

MODEL: Eliana Rubin — she/her

Three of Swords

TURMOIL, HEARTBREAK, GRIEF, HURT, DISAPPOINTMENT

The Three of Swords often appears when you're experiencing an emotional disappointment, like heartbreak or betrayal. It reveals the harsh truths about difficult situations that you may not be ready to face. These can be painful times, especially when they come about unexpectedly. The sharp edge of the Swords causes sadness, pain, grief, and bad vibes all around—so how do you recover? Now is not the time to sulk—release this person, event, or feeling, and start your recovery. Dwelling in the past will only make things worse when you need to heal. The Three of Swords reminds us that we need to take these kinds of experiences and use them to develop. To know and face all the difficult emotions that come with pain and hurt is to come out with the tools needed to move forward as a stronger, better version of you. Self-love, forgiveness, and trust in the process are what you need to get through this.

REVERSE: Your inner critic is drowning out your self-love, making you question yourself. Remember that negative self-talk really brings you down, and you're hypersensitive to it right now. If you are feeling emotionally fragile, it's a good moment to spend time mending your heart.

THINGS TO CONSIDER: Cry. Let it all out! Crying makes you feel better. What we perceive isn't always the same as what is actually happening around us. Step back and analyze the situation: consider everyone involved and their feelings and/or situation. Know that you are not alone.

Four of Swords

REST, RECUPERATION, STILLNESS, MEDITATION

The Four of Swords indicates that it's now time to retreat and rest from whatever is bringing you down, whether that's stress, illness, trauma, heartache, or anything else. When this card appears in your reading, spend lots of time building up your mental and emotional strength. Alone time is crucial in this moment—finding stillness and solitude can often lead to clarity, which is exactly what this card prescribes! Remember, the body and mind need time to restore and rebuild before you experience burnout—once you are in the middle of it, it can be too late.

REVERSE: You are exhausted and burnt out. It's time to reevaluate your obligations because they're piling up and draining you. Allow for rest and seclusion, and go within to restore yourself.

THINGS TO CONSIDER: What does your ideal day of relaxation look like? Consider trying meditation. If it is difficult for you to take a break, ask yourself why. What is holding you back?

MODEL: East — she/her/they

Five of Swords

SELF-DESTRUCTION, DEFEAT, LOSS, CONFLICT, RECONCILIATION, CONVICTIONS

The Five of Swords reveals defeat, whether a personal battle lost or something that has not gone to plan. When you're in conflict with others, you may feel compelled to win the argument or prove you're right, but remember that not all conflicts are worth what they cost. You should use this understanding to consider compromise rather than further arguments. Don't be tempted to win at all costs, since many times the loss is not worth the victory. This card asks you to consider your values and integrity—do the means outweigh the end? Remember, dwelling on losses will only lead to more distress and turmoil. Move on when you can.

REVERSE: Unresolved conflict may be getting under your skin, and you may be harboring some resentment. This is making it hard for you to move on, and now is the time to finally address what's bothering you so you can begin to unburden yourself.

THINGS TO CONSIDER: Choose your battles. When dealing with a loss, notice that you need to make space for yourself to heal.

MODEL: Alyssa Lizardo — she/her

Six of Swords

HOPE, RELIEF, COMPANIONSHIP, MOVING ON (TRAVEL)

The Six of Swords appears when you're finally shifting away from a difficult situation—the worst is behind you and you can now pick yourself up and begin moving forward. This card, at its simplest, urges you to shed what doesn't serve you. You've realized the pain and difficulty and asked for help to move through this transition. It's challenging to leave baggage behind, but remember that you are heading toward a better and brighter future. The Six of Swords is reassuring you that it's okay to move on.

REVERSE: All signs are pointing toward you leaving a difficult situation, but it feels so hard to do. You may feel hesitant and like you'll never be ready to let go, but remember that you are only being harmed by staying in this situation. You don't want to stunt your growth. This is a good time to consider your worth and remember that nobody values you as much as you value yourself.

THINGS TO CONSIDER: What baggage are you carrying around with you right now? What is weighing you down and preventing you from living to your greatest potential? Is it worth it holding on to that thing?

MODELS: Jennie Eisenhower — she/her;
Sara Neville — she/her

Seven of Swords

DISHONESTY, LIES, INSECURITY, WITHHOLDING, STRATEGY

The Seven of Swords indicates dishonesty, whether your own or that of another party. This card asks you to reassess any secretive behaviors you may be exhibiting. Are these secrets keeping you safe from something or are you harboring them for someone else's sake? It's time to analyze what you are keeping to yourself—or maybe even *from* yourself. The Seven of Swords not only suggests a secret being kept or dishonest activity, but it can also bring your attention to a truth you don't want to face or maybe something you haven't considered but that has been influencing you without your knowledge. If you are the one being tricked, stay on the lookout and try being a little more aware of strange situations. Greed, thoughtless behavior, and impulsiveness are traits of the Seven of Swords and can be easily spotted.

REVERSE: **This card could signify betrayal. This may be a good time to take a step back and analyze your relationships and how they are impacting your life.**

THINGS TO CONSIDER: **Ask yourself this: Are you lying or keeping secrets, and if so, is it hurting you or anyone involved? Write your pros and cons for justifying your sneaky behavior. Is it a selfish decision or rooted in good intentions? Try giving yourself some alone time to think about why you are staying in this situation or what is keeping you here. There are no wrong answers, only reflection.**

MODEL: STEFF — they/them

Eight of Swords

RESTRICTION, POWERLESS, STUCK

The Eight of Swords asks you to consider what is holding you back. You may be feeling trapped and stuck in a mental prison with your thoughts and limiting beliefs. The Eight of Swords reminds us that we have the power to get out of this rut that we're stuck in. Don't allow yourself to wallow in it—remember, you are not powerless! You feel tied up and sightless behind your blindfold, but you just need to remind yourself that you can be the one to take it off. If you've been putting something off, now is the time to stop ignoring it and start dealing with it. Once it's done, you'll think, *Well, that wasn't so bad after all!* This card wants you to open your eyes and face the truth—what's keeping you from moving forward? Are you a hostage of your own mindset? Beware of your outward behaviors as well—don't take what is bothering you out on anyone else. When you're stuck in a hard situation, it can be too easy to blame others for your misfortune.

REVERSE: Your inner dialogue may be telling you you're not worthy of fortune or a happier, healthier life. You don't feel

deserving, so you don't hope for better. This is a good time to reevaluate your self-worth. Who gave you the idea that you're not good enough?

THINGS TO CONSIDER: **Where did this start? What is the root of what's causing you to feel unable to make a move? Reflect on how you got here and what is holding you back. Consider life once you are past this mess. Does it look happy? Sad? Can it be a little bit of both?**

MODEL: Camille Leon (aka Allison Carvalho) — she/her

Nine of Swords

DESPAIR, ANXIETY, ANGUISH

The Nine of Swords suggests you're seriously going through it, and as a repercussion, it's keeping you up at night and disturbing your peace. Your anguish is feeding the fear-monster deep within your soul. Anxiety could be triggered, with despair and agony flowing through every vein in your body and worry taking up all the real estate in your brain. This is absolutely *not* a very welcome card, but acknowledging this full-on pain is the first step toward getting rid of these uncomfortable feelings. The only way to end such negativity is to go through it, rather than by trying to shoo it away. Even if you feel increasingly powerless and useless at this time, know that you are valid and deserve happiness just as much as anybody else! Know that you are not alone when it comes to these unpleasant feelings and emotions. Talking it out can really help turn things around. Working through your feelings is a wonderful way to conquer them. Just by saying them out loud and letting them leave your body—literally releasing the fears and doubts—will make you feel lighter. Don't be afraid to seek help, either. Whether by seeing a therapist or just connecting with a stranger on the Internet who may also be going through similar things, sharing your inner thoughts and issues with someone who will listen can be really freeing.

REVERSE: Your negative thinking is getting the best of you, and it's hard for you to see past it. You may be keeping all of this inside, reinforcing an endless loop of negative thinking. This might be a good time to reach out to others, like a trusted friend or a therapist, for help.

THINGS TO CONSIDER: Journal all your fears out. Talk to someone you trust about how you feel. Find other people who may be feeling what you are, like members of a support group or a friend—it feels good to have proof that you aren't alone. Visualize your fears leaving your mind. Do this by imagining a safe and happy place, where nothing can bother you. Go there when you are down.

MODEL: Maddy Wager — they/them

Ten of Swords

ROCK BOTTOM, RUIN, LOSS

The Ten of Swords may be the worst card in the deck—it 100 percent symbolizes rock bottom, nothing left to lose. The good news? You've experienced the worst of the worst, so the only path is forward and through! This card may hit you hard, as you may not be expecting such betrayal or backstabbing, and it can send you into a downward spiral as you contemplate the painful and inevitable ending you are about to face. It can feel as though your world is crumbling around you. But take heart! Now that you're at the bottom, the only way left is back up! Do you stay down and continue to mope around on the floor, or do you pick yourself back up and start anew, continuing life instead of being pitied? Luckily, the Ten of Swords has a kind of double meaning; it encourages letting go and accepting the current circumstances presented to you, quite literally signifying the end of something. Use this card as a reminder that you can learn from this negative experience and all of the pain wasn't for nothing. It is a chance to evolve.

REVERSE: Resisting endings makes things worse and delays your recovery. You may be in denial about an end that's already happened, so you are holding on to the pain of it. It's time to reach out for support and work on feeling grounded and connected to yourself again.

THINGS TO CONSIDER: Take a step back from the drama for a second. Breathe. Identify the root causes of this wild situation and really ask yourself: Am I here for the thrill, or is it truly something that I care about?

MODEL: James Manzano — any pronouns

Page of Swords

CURIOUS, IDEALISTIC, ENTHUSIASTIC

The Page of Swords represents a young, idealistic mind that's brimming with excitement and eagerness to learn, explore, and discover new things! Curiosity overcomes the Page of Swords, but it's often accompanied by stubbornness and a tendency to become detached from reality. Remember, it can be exciting to jump in, but you're a novice. Be careful not to ignore the possibility of trouble or the challenges that lie ahead. Taking risks and following the heart are things the Page of Swords has mastered, but that doesn't mean they always succeed! Keep that beginner's mindset to maintain optimism and enthusiasm, but try not to stray too far away from the realistic. Remain present and be wary of making hasty decisions.

REVERSE: You may have difficulty following through on your new ideas or are keeping these ideas to yourself for fear of rejection. Remember that you are a novice and it's okay not to know everything! You're learning!

THINGS TO CONSIDER: If you don't understand something or want to do it your way, be open to learning rather than

taking offense. Allow yourself to be corrected and learn from it! Look at your situation from a logical perspective. Is your goal attainable, and if so, to what extent? Take a break from the people you clash with or try finding middle ground with them. Start something new you've had your eye on.

MODEL: Mintzu Chen/陳岷慈 — they/them/他

Knight of Swords

STUBBORN, DETERMINED, IMPULSIVE

The Knight of Swords is like a tornado that tears through your life and upends everything, with no regard for the damage they are causing. They are in it for the thrill, but usually unaware of people, their feelings, or the effect their actions have on others. This stubborn person wants to do it their way, and trouble tends to follow. The intense energy of this card will definitely show you a good time, but probably at a high cost—whether that is your morals, someone else's feelings, or anything that can be betrayed. While the Knight of Swords may be intelligent and well-intentioned in other ways, they often have a hard time being aware of sensitivity and vulnerability. This is a very action-oriented card, perhaps signifying a very urgent situation is coming up or warning you to think it through instead of diving headfirst into action without a plan. Going into a situation blindly is what this card basically stands for, and in most cases it's urging you *not* to do this! You may have the confidence and bravery behind you, but don't act foolishly.

REVERSE: Slow down—you don't want to risk burning out right now. You may be feeling scattered, acting impulsively, and harming people along the way.

THINGS TO CONSIDER: Be aware of the people around you and how you impact them with your decisions. How are your actions influencing their lives? Find the root of your intolerance and try to see things from someone else's perspective. Have a plan before diving in headfirst if you are involved in a conflict.

MODEL: Niko Nada — they/them

Queen of Swords

INTUITION, LOGIC, HONESTY

The Queen of Swords is someone who knows the boundary between the emotional and logical realms very well. They are usually intelligent, very in touch with their intuition, and use honesty as their best policy. Because they generally lack emotion, they are able to see things with the mind alone, without the heart getting in the way. The Queen of Swords can take the heart out of a specific situation or, on the flip side, can show when a little heart is needed. Showing emotions is by no means a sign of weakness, and this card calls for a time to check in and find out where both your head and your heart are. Detaching from your heart for a moment may bring clarity that you couldn't find before, and vice versa.

REVERSE: **You may come across as dismissive or cold, seemingly lacking emotional maturity. Don't let your negative emotions get the best of you.**

THINGS TO CONSIDER: **Be honest with yourself about your doubts. Try ditching your feelings when thinking about the situation. Imagine removing your heart and think about the log-**

istics. Or perhaps you're facing the opposite problem: Is practicality getting in the way of what your heart wants? What do you see when you remove your personal feelings from the equation? Take a step back and check in with your habits—are you living in a fantasy world or are you being practical in the way you're living your life?

MODEL: Amber Berkins — she/her

King of Swords

ETHICAL, JUST, COMMUNICATIVE

The King of Swords embodies powerful knowledge, a great deal of rationality, and the use of ethics and logic to power through life. They often come in the form of an authority figure or someone who excels in their profession, making them intelligent as well as trustworthy. As in nearly all Swords-related situations, though, emotion is not present here. The King of Swords' lack of emotion allows them to make decisions and judge based on ethics and logic alone. Clear communication is always a given with this type of figure, even if they are unable to express themselves with emotions.

REVERSE: **Don't let your ego get in the way—being in a position of power or authority can sometimes blur your perception of self, and not for the better.**

THINGS TO CONSIDER: **If your emotions are feeling a bit out of control, channel the energy of the King of Swords. Detach your emotions from the situation and look at it from a logical point of view. Try new ways of communicating if you are having trouble getting your ideas across.**

MODEL: Wes Graham — he/they

Ace of Pentacles
II
IV
VI
VII
VIII
IX

Page of Pentacles

Pentacles

Knight of Pentacles

Queen of Pentacles

King of Pentacles

Ace of Pentacles

PROSPERITY, NEW BEGINNINGS, GROWTH

The Ace of Pentacles signals prosperous beginnings, leading the way in stable and steady progress toward your goals and endeavors. It can represent a new job, hobby, or chance to bring an idea to fruition. You are now in a safe space to grow and thrive with confidence, and it's never been a better time to put down new roots! But be warned, this card is not a freebie. Use this as a reminder that working hard to achieve what you want is necessary for success. Take this time to really map out your future plans—right now you are in a position to see all that is coming, which gives you extra time to really think about what you want your end goal to be. Open your mind to new ways of growing in the direction that suits you. And if you are in a position to share your prosperity and benefit others in need with your new efforts, do so! Give back to your community or to your friends and family. The Ace of Pentacles is a reminder that when things are looking up for you, you shouldn't keep it all for yourself.

REVERSE: You may be lacking in forward thinking at this time and having difficulties coming up with plans of execution.

THINGS TO CONSIDER: What do you need to do for yourself personally in order to reach your goals? How can you get there? What does working hard look like to you? How can you share the success and benefits with the people around you? Consider starting small and go from there.

Two of Pentacles

BALANCE, HARMONIOUS CHANGE

The Two of Pentacles signifies a much-needed change, whether you want it or not, and speaks to the art of cultivating balance when adapting to new norms that may arise. This could come at a time when you feel like you're juggling priorities and responsibilities—where is the fine line between efficiently managing something versus losing control? If you feel extremely busy and it seems like things are falling apart, it may be a good idea to take a break and start your search for harmony. Getting caught up in the day-to-day can often blur your view of the big picture, so it's okay to take some time to recenter yourself. The Two of Pentacles reminds us to be patient, flexible, and adaptable when dealing with many responsibilities at once and to accept change even if it throws our plans off a little.

REVERSE: **You may be feeling out of balance and overcommitted. The struggle to find harmony in your life is making things a little stressful.**

THINGS TO CONSIDER: **Find a part of your life that may not be getting the attention it needs. Take a break from your normal activities to nurture a responsibility or aspect of your life that you have been ignoring.**

MODEL: Divya L. — she/her

Three of Pentacles

PASSION, ACCOMPLISHMENT, COLLABORATION

The Three of Pentacles is a card of passion, usually around your work or career. This card urges you to not be afraid of risk if you are feeling less experienced, whether alone or in a group. Everyone will always have something different to bring to the table, and when your heart is behind it, you truly will have an advantage in terms of your skills and insight. Trust yourself and your abilities and those of others around you. Though failure may seem inevitable, don't let it deter you. It can be a learning experience, preparing you for next time. Now is not the moment to doubt yourself. Collaboration on projects is important, and having a strong foundation with the folx you are working with can bring your endeavor to the next level.

REVERSE: **You may be feeling out of sync with those around you, or like you are experiencing difficulties in working closely with others. Take time to reassess the original purpose of your collaboration and get on the same page as your teammates.**

THINGS TO CONSIDER: **What is your dream? Identify it, then write a simplified list of steps you can take to get there or outline where to begin. Ask yourself: are you passionate about what you are doing? Take baby steps if you feel doubtful. Small victories can lead to big achievements. What more can you learn to further your skill in something you love doing?**

MODELS: Fred Rivera — he/him; KB — they/them; Nan Peña — she/her

Four of Pentacles

POSSESSIONS, POWER, SCARCITY, GREED, CONSERVATISM

The Four of Pentacles warns us not to get too caught up in our possessions, physical or metaphorical! Becoming possessive or controlling isn't really a good look. When you lose sight of other important things, such as family, friends, and other values, you may very well start to find yourself isolated. Stability is often perceived as a prized achievement in our society, but that doesn't mean it has to become the center of your world. There is absolutely no need to get so wrapped up in your success or your belongings that you become oblivious to everything else.

REVERSE: When the Four of Pentacles appears reversed, it may mean that you've started to realize you've spent too much time placing value on your material possessions. You may be distancing yourself from them. Your love for *things* may have turned to greed, and it's glaringly obvious that you're neglecting your relationships in favor of material items.

THINGS TO CONSIDER: Examine your relationship with material things. What is keeping you so attached? Try having a

day where you are away from possession and are not in control, like a nature day in the woods or a beach day with no cell service. Accept that you are not the supreme being.

MODEL: Madi Bowman — she/they

Five of Pentacles

HARDSHIP, LOSS, SADNESS

The Five of Pentacles represents a time of hardship and loss, likely in material form. You may be feeling as though you are in deep trouble, and in order to pull yourself out of this rut of devastation you must not be afraid to seek outside help. Often when we struggle, we are so lost in our own worry that the concept of outside help rests undisturbed in our blind spot. Even if it feels like you aren't going to recover from whatever grim situation is afoot, and that all hope is totally lost, there will always be some opportunity to turn things around. And it might not be easy.

REVERSE: **The Five of Pentacles reversed can indicate that this time of financial hardship is coming to an end. Maybe you've** secured a new job or found help in some other way. This can also indicate that you're placing too much value on wealth—sometimes it's okay to have just a little, so long as you're fulfilled and safe in other ways.

THINGS TO CONSIDER: Don't be afraid to ask for help. Reflect on what brought you to this moment and meditate on finding hope and peace to get you out of these hard times. If asking for help is difficult for you, try writing your problems down first. Seeing it on paper—a different perspective than when the issue is inside your head—might give you the push you need to materialize the next steps.

MODELS: Terri Meade — she/they;
Clark Napasindayao — he/him

Six of Pentacles

GENEROSITY, APPRECIATION, PROSPERITY

The Six of Pentacles is a special card to pull. It is a card of all manner of wealth, whether you already have it or are in need of it. This card urges you to be generous and share your resources. Be grateful when someone helps you out, or if the situation is reversed, be grateful that you have the means to help someone out when they are down. Giving with no strings attached is the right way to go when it comes to this card, as sharing with ulterior motives can cause hostility and dependency. This type of controlling mindset is unproductive. If you are in the position to share some of your wealth, whatever that may look like for you, do so gladly! Pay reparations, help raise money for someone's top surgery, take in someone to mentor, or share resources and other nonmaterial things like love, knowledge, support, and affirmations. The Six of Pentacles wants you to give back to your community, because if we all have each other's backs, then we will always be taken care of. Something to keep in mind, though, is to be conscious of your giving. Even if your intentions are good, know when to stop if it is affecting your well-being. A good tip is to give what you can. The Six of Pentacles can also represent your dependency on money or material things, or even a person. It may be time to step back and examine your relationship with money or something else of value and look for ways to find balance away from material things.

REVERSE: **While you may be so generous to others, are you being generous to yourself? When the Six of Pentacles appears reversed it's reminding you to take care of yourself too—sometimes you give so much to others, only to be disappointed when you get nothing in return. Check this—if you're donating to mutual aid or other community projects, make sure you're doing this because you *want* to, not because you want something from it, like internet clout, acknowledgment, etc. . . . Maybe you're struggling yourself and wish that others would help you out. Be aware not to stretch yourself too far in your commitments to helping others; it's important to put yourself first at times too.**

THINGS TO CONSIDER: **Identify yourself in the card: Are you the giver or the beggar? Don't be afraid to ask for help, whether by choosing an organization to share funds with or asking your friends for assistance. What is holding you so closely to your material things? Do you need these things to live? Can you**

spare anything at all? Keep this in mind: There's room for all of us at the top.

MODELS: Madeline Graves — she/her/they/them;
Nico/Aura — he/him, she/her;
Kyle Parker — he/him/she/her/they/them

Seven of Pentacles

STEADY PROGRESS, PATIENCE, GROWTH

Remember that it's totally worth it to put in work and energy in order to see your big picture goals come true. It may not feel fruitful in the moment, but this energy is valuable, nonetheless. If you're feeling discouraged by your day-to-day activities, step back and try to envision your big picture. Just be careful, as sometimes you put a ton of time and energy into something only to realize it wasn't worth the effort. Carefully evaluate your long-term views and see what seems most beneficial for you. The Seven of Pentacles indicates that you might be having trouble spotting the light at the end of the tunnel. You feel overworked and under-accomplished, but that is just simply not true. Remember that not every big show of effort yields immediate results.

REVERSE: **Take a long hard look at where you're investing your time and energy—is it still making you happy? Make sure you're using your resources wisely. You may be focusing on a big-picture goal that isn't currently bringing you joy—figure out why not. Are you spending too much time dawdling and not making any forward progress? Are you using resources effectively? Remember, you don't need to trudge through something that is making you miserable. Goalposts can change, and that's okay.**

THINGS TO CONSIDER: **What are you investing your energy in? Does it seem draining? Are your old goals still attainable? Take a moment to write down some new goals if not—remember that "resolutions" can be made at any time, not just during the New Year, and they are malleable.**

MODEL: Adrian M — they/them

Eight of Pentacles

LEARNING, SKILL, WORK ETHIC

The Eight of Pentacles is a card of progress. It is a reminder that what you are learning today will be of importance to you later in life. This can apply to anything—your career, your hobbies, your identity, or your sexuality, to name a few. Now is really the time to pay attention and home in on your craft, because knowledge is power! This card can also represent a busy time in your life, during which you may feel overwhelmed with work and learning. Let this be a pep talk to give it your all, even when it comes to the boring and tedious stuff. However, if you are totally miserable, you may consider switching paths. The Eight of Pentacles not only represents cultivating a good work ethic and retaining knowledge, but urges those who aren't happy with what they're doing in life to make a change.

REVERSE: You're focusing more on developing your very best version of yourself. However, use this as a reminder to not be too hard on yourself. You're growing, and growth inevitably also means setbacks are looming. Don't resist them, and focus instead on persevering. Remember to be adaptable and self-loving when

you fail. As long as your goals are realistic and you're not striving for absolute perfection, you're on the right path, no matter how many twists and turns it may have.

THINGS TO CONSIDER: Consider your personal growth alongside the growth of your skills. How have you changed as a person with the knowledge and skills you have now? How has working toward something you enjoy changed you? On a scale of one to ten, how much are you loving what you do? What is something you've always wanted to learn about?

MODEL: A.C. Williams — they/them

Nine of Pentacles

PROSPERITY, LUXURY, COMFORT

The Nine of Pentacles is a card of abundance. It represents a bountiful time in your life and encourages you to spoil yourself a bit to celebrate your success! This is a time to sit back, relax, and look at what you've built for yourself and what you've been working toward. It's okay to take a break and bask in your achievement, but even if things are looking up, you have to remember not to blow all your money in one place. Even though you may have the means to revel a little doesn't mean you need to go all out. Being mindful and showing moderation are necessary parts of enjoying your prosperity when it comes to the Nine of Pentacles. We are also reminded to be grateful for the things we have right now. Things are good, so take time to appreciate them.

REVERSE: Reflect on your sense of self-worth and value. You might be feeling like you're not enough, but remember that you're the only person who will invest heavily into you. Take a moment for some personal time and indulge yourself in a bit of luxury if you can spare. This doesn't have to be a monetary indulgence, but just remember that you're worth it if it is!

THINGS TO CONSIDER: What can you celebrate right now? Take a moment to be grateful for the people and things around you and to acknowledge everything that got you where you are today. Know when to stop spoiling yourself though, as moderation is key. Be open to sharing your experiences around your success.

MODEL: Marina Brock — she/her

Ten of Pentacles

WEALTH, HAPPINESS, FULFILLMENT

The Ten of Pentacles represents a time filled with happiness and completion, a time when you have everything you need. Through your journey, you've accumulated experiences, knowledge, and connections, resulting in success, security, and stability. You no longer have to work in survival mode now that you are fully equipped to navigate life without your old fears and doubts weighing you down. And you are strong enough to handle any hiccups moving forward. Confidence abounds and you can finally rest!

REVERSE: The Ten of Pentacles reversed can ask you why you feel this need for stability. Is it helping you, or are you just settling for comfort when you long for something else? Remember that sometimes becoming accustomed to a certain lifestyle, especially with an emphasis on money, may end up feeling like you never have enough. You may find yourself lusting after more, when in reality you already have more than enough.

THINGS TO CONSIDER: Journal. Write and reflect on your journey and what brought you here. Acknowledge your support system and thank them.

MODELS: Talaya Banks — she/they;
Mara Hasenstaub — she/her; Joe Gualtiere — he/him

Page of Pentacles

EAGER TO LEARN, DEDICATED, RESPONSIBLE

The Page of Pentacles represents a novice, eager to take the next step and make their dreams come true. They are dedicated to acquiring knowledge, willing to learn, and ready to prove reliability, even if their skills are lacking. This card presents us with the go-ahead to take on a new hobby or start a project. It's the perfect time to pursue those next exciting steps in learning something new. The Page of Pentacles also reminds us that time and perseverance are crucial when learning. With patience and hard work you will have the potential to go far. The road before you is long and will be filled with many important learning experiences—be sure to take notes.

REVERSE: You're starting to explore a new project, but you don't quite have enough of a plan to move forward into it yet, and

that's fine! Give yourself space to plan this journey and refocus.

THINGS TO CONSIDER: What are the next steps for you as you journey into something new? Write down your dreams or end goals and tape them somewhere you will see every day.

MODEL: Charissa Kow — she/her

Knight of Pentacles

LOYAL, HARDWORKING, TRUSTWORTHY

The Knight of Pentacles comes in the form of a dedicated person, one who knows responsibility and can get through any challenge life brings them. Their work ethic is what's really being showcased here, as they bring passion and a committed touch to any project they are presented with. But when practicality and logic are necessary in working toward a goal, dullness and stubbornness can take over. Just remember that hard work is worth it in the end, and this may be a reminder to you that even if tedious work can be tiresome and boring, the outcome has the potential to be great. The Knight of Pentacles may be a sign that you need to buckle down and really give an upcoming project or task your all. Giving up is not recommended here; no matter how difficult or mundane the task, be strong and resilient rather than lazy and inflexible. The Knight of Pentacles can act as a subtle reminder to consider all the hardworking folx around you.

REVERSE: **This centers on establishing routines, however mundane they may be, in order to focus on maintaining your successes. Sometimes you get carried away by your grand plans and leave the basics behind. Or perhaps it's the other side of the coin—you're far too caught up in the daily routine and feel stifled and stuck. Whichever it is, the message is the same—balance.**

THINGS TO CONSIDER: **Is there something you've been putting off that you've been dreading? Write a list of positive outcomes for a boring task and see if that changes your perspective on it. Try thanking the Knights of Pentacles in your life for their hard work. Take a moment to feel and acknowledge your gratitude toward all of the pioneers who work daily to make this world a better and safer place for queer people and for those who are dedicated to the well-being of the community.**

MODELS: Asim — they/them/he/his

Queen of Pentacles

HOMELY, GENEROUS, WHOLESOME

The Queen of Pentacles is someone who prides themself on their loving and nurturing nature. The Queen will totally take care of you, especially if you're feeling ill or down in the dumps. This person is a huge fan of simplicity and frugality when it comes to money and lifestyle and generally a self-made hard worker. They also generally lead a modest life, devoid of worldly distractions, which allows them to be fully present. The Queen of Pentacles encourages smart thinking and future considerations when dealing with financial or material things. Think long-term investments right now rather than frivolous and spontaneous pursuits. And when it comes to being there for someone, be generous and caring. These are things we can learn from the Queen of Pentacles.

REVERSE: Whether you are short in money or short in morality, the Queen of Pentacles in reverse symbolizes a time where you may be feeling possessive and mistrustful of others. You might feel like you're losing your grip or slipping away from the things that bring you comfort.

THINGS TO CONSIDER: **Take care of someone rather than letting them take care of you. Be conscious of where your money is being spent or where you're wearing yourself too thin.**

MODEL: Camellia Jahanshahi — she/her

King of Pentacles

WEALTH, STABILITY, DISCIPLINE

The King of Pentacles is a person who is successful in attracting, managing, and maintaining wealth in a level-headed manner, but who can have issues letting people in. They are calm, thoughtful, and reasonable when dealing with money and business-related situations. When it comes to providing others with advice or guidance pertaining to money issues and work-related matters, they shine. However, they do not let their personal life get in the way, which can be both a good and a bad thing.

This card invites the idea of being smart with your wealth, and reminds you not to forget that a balance between work and life is crucial. What can you do to get to a steady and stable point in your life when it comes to your career or your means versus the health of your personal life? At what point does it matter if you're working for success or for happiness, and can it be both? These are important things to think about if you are in the position of the King.

REVERSE: With the title of King comes power, and with power comes abuse. Falling into patterns of greed and dishonesty can easily be a struggle that you'll face when in this position.

THINGS TO CONSIDER: Is your job taking a toll on your personal happiness, and if it is, is it worth it? Enjoy your wealth, but be smart with how you use it. Share your knowledge and experience with others who are just starting out.

MODEL: Bug Cru — they/them

Model Credits and Card Art Descriptions

All art descriptions reflect the pronouns of the models who were kind enough to participate in this project.

0, The Fool

MODEL: Alett | they/she | Texas | @alett.t

A person stands unaware at the edge of a cliff. They hold a knapsack slung over her shoulder and a flower in their hand. A small dog bounces at her feet.

1, The Magician

MODEL: Jul | they/them | Brooklyn, NY | @julchateau

A person stands with one arm pointed upward and one pointed down. A sword, a wand, a cup, and a coin rest on the table in front of them. They are surrounded by flowers.

2, The High Priestess

MODEL: Chala. | they/he | Brooklyn, NY (Lenapehoking)

A person sits on a throne with pomegranates behind them and pillars, one black and one white, on either side. He holds a book in their hand and there is a crescent moon at his feet.

3, The Empress

MODEL: jae | they/them/theirs | Lenapehoking (Brooklyn, NY) | @jae.tav @zzmoonshine

A person sits on cushions with a crown of stars on their head. They are surrounded by nature. In their hand they hold a scepter. The transgender symbol is etched into a stone heart on the ground beside them.

4, The Emperor

MODEL: Taylor Tucker | he/him | West Hartford, CT | @totsmcgee123

A person sits on a throne decorated with four rams' heads. In one hand he holds a stick with the trans symbol on its end, and in the other he holds an orb. Behind him are jagged mountains.

5, The Hierophant

MODELS: Albert Rios | he/him | Oklahoma City, OK | @Albz86
Alex Luciano | she/her | Richmond, VA | @g_a_l_e_x
TK | he/him | Powhatan Confederacy | @tkartdesign @amerikanastudio

A person sits on a throne between two decorated pillars. In one hand he holds a scepter and on the other he holds up two fingers. Two worshippers appear in the foreground.

6, The Lovers

MODELS: pau venadito | they/them | @paupau_ux
Valentine Darling | they/them | Olympia, WA | @recovery.disco
Luz Miranda | she/they | Chicago, IL | @youremynirvana

Two lovers stand beneath an angel, who is looking down on them. Behind them are two trees—one ripe with pomegranates and the other on fire.

7, The Chariot

MODEL: Karli Miller | they/them | Allentown, PA | @chronicallykarli @thatwheelchairmermaid

A person sits in a wheelchair decorated with rainbows. A rainbow descends from the sky. Two dogs sit loyally at their feet.

8, Strength

MODEL: Danny Gee | he/him | Pacific Northwest, U.S.A. | @DannyGJr

A person stands with a lion, petting it while it is resting its head in his hands. Behind him is a rainbow.

9, The Hermit

MODEL: Heather | she/her | Richmond, VA | @hldoubleu

A person stands on top of a mountain, holding a light in front of her. She is holding a walking stick in the other hand and looking forward.

10, Wheel of Fortune

MODEL: Tara Shea Burke | she/her | Richmond, VA | @tarashea

A giant wheel is at the center of the card. A snake and an Anubis are on the outside. In the corners of the card are a woman, a bull, a bird, and a cat.

11, Justice

MODEL: Vico Ortiz | they/him/she | Tongva Land (Los Angeles, CA) | @puertoricaninja

A person sits on a stone slab with a sword in one hand and scales in the other. They wear a woven crown on their head.

12, The Hanged Man

MODEL: Eli Bird | he/him | Winnipeg, MB, Canada | @buhbird

A person wearing a pink triangle on their shirt hangs upside down. One of his feet is tied to a branch and the other is free.

13, Death

MODELS: Ricky Tyler | he/they | Ridgewood, NY | @boy.cupid_
Jarred Daniels | he/him | Grand Rapids, MI | @saynooo_tobasics
Grace Duong | she/her | Philadelphia, PA | @grace.duong
@mysticmondays

A skeleton rides a white horse with a black flag in his hand. Beneath him, a person lies on the ground, dead. In front of him, two townspeople beg to be spared.

14, Temperance

MODEL: matty | they/them | New York, NY | @mattycakes16

A person wearing a dress with one leg poking out pours a rainbow from one cup to another. Behind them is a pink triangle, and on either side of them are jagged mountains and flowers.

15, The Devil

MODELS: Malek Ansari | they/them | Chicago, IL | @ansari_not_sorry
Constance Shumaker | she/her | Richmond, VA | @ConnieTroversial
Angie Cooper | she/her | Richmond, VA | @totheriver

A horned creature crouches on a pedestal. On either side of her, two people appear standing in chains.

16, The Tower

MODELS: Luis Miguel Sosa | he/him | Miami, FL | @sosastarlinggg
Danny Brito | he/him | Miami, FL | @dannybrito

A tower stands in stormy weather, struck by lightning, with flames shooting out of the windows. Two people plunge from the tower toward jagged ground.

17, The Star

MODEL: Riylan M. | she/her | Brooklyn, NY | @riylanmills

A person kneels at the edge of a pond and pours water from containers in both of her hands. Behind her, the scenery is lush and there is a rainbow depicting the Philadelphia flag.

18, The Moon

A full moon shines between two towers. In the foreground is a shimmering pool of water, from which a crayfish exits. Two dogs stand in the grass and howl at the moon.

19, The Sun

A large sun shines in the sky. A child sits on top of a white unicorn with rainbows and flowers surrounding her.

20, Judgment

MODELS: Edrian Pangilinan | he/him | San Diego, CA | @edrianpenguino
Lee Ellen Fanning | she/her | New York, NY | #leeellenfanningwhoisnotoninstagram
Melody Lee Rosa | she/her | Brooklyn, NY | @waterbruja
Alex Teschel | she/they | Richmond VA | @tesch.tif
Meg Thompson | she/her | New York, NY | @meg_thompson
Sofia Kon. | she/they | Athens, Greece | @rosyair

An angel appears in the sky, blowing a trumpet with a lesbian pride flag attached to it. Five people appear in the foreground raising their arms to the angel.

21, The World

MODEL: Miranda | she/her | "Vancouver," Coast Salish Territory | @beefiebitch

The person in the center of the wreath stands balanced on one leg. The four outside figures represent the four fixed signs of the Zodiac.

Ace of Wands

A hand is coming out of a puff of cloud, holding onto a blossoming wand. Behind it lies a vast desert of sand and a large white structure sitting on top of a hill. There is a rainbow of the asexual flag colors sitting on the horizon.

Two of Wands

MODEL: Elsa G. aka Wild Black | she/they | Toronto, ON | @wildblackmusic

A person stands on a balcony, holding the world in the palm of their right hand and a wand in their left. She looks out into the distance, contemplating their next big move.

Three of Wands

MODEL: Oran Colwell | he/him | Effingham, IL | @orancolwell

A person is standing and looking out into the vast land beyond him. Two wands are firmly planted in the ground behind the person and a third is in his right hand.

Four of Wands

MODELS: Nic Charlie Perez | she/her | Richmond, VA | @niccharlieperez @paintedattheseams

Rachel Brown | she/her | Richmond, VA

Two people are celebrating, holding flowers above their heads. Behind them is a grand castle and before them are four wands sticking up from the ground, topped with flowers.

Five of Wands

MODELS: Leo | they/them | Inglewood, CA | @_leo.sun

Nina Alexander | she/her | Oakland, CA | @broccoli.irl

Jini Valence | she/they | Richmond, VA | @jiniandtonic
Bailey Sell | he/him | Grand Rapids, MI | @transfigureprintco
Kevin August | he/him | Boston, MA | @thekeving

Five people disagree over something, and each holds their wand above their head, ready to strike.

Six of Wands

MODELS: Chess Needham | he/him | Richmond, VA | @chessieneedham
Ash Molesso | she/her | Richmond, VA | @ashleymolesso
Cassie Carrasco | she/they | Austin, TX

A person rides atop a caped horse through a small crowd of people, a wand topped with a wreath of flowers in their hand. Five wands float behind them.

Seven of Wands

MODEL: Imani Russell | they/them | Brooklyn, NY | @imanithecowboy

A person is standing on top of a hill, holding a wand and fighting off six other wands that reach up toward them.

Eight of Wands

Eight wands are slicing through the air from the top left to the bottom right, seemingly as fast as lightning.

Nine of Wands

MODEL: Rico Castillo | they/them | Los Angeles, CA | @quasarico

A person stands holding onto a wand, with eight more wands placed behind them.

Ten of Wands

MODEL: Maxx Rayne | she/her | San Diego, CA | @maxxrayne

A person is carrying a bundle of wands outside of a town, and she has almost reached her destination. She is struggling to carry everything but is hopeful and looking forward to delivering and releasing the weight she is carrying.

Page of Wands

MODEL: Natasha R. Johnson | she/her/unicorn | Brooklyn, NY |

@daily_n_spiration

A person holds a single wand upright, looking toward it. Behind her is a desert and sand dunes. Swirls of the genderqueer flag float in the sky behind them.

Knight of Wands

MODEL: Toni Rowe | she/her | London, England

A person sits on her horse, holding a wand in her right hand. Behind her is a desert and towering sand dunes. An asexual flag rainbow is in the sky.

Queen of Wands

MODEL: Riley M. | she/they | Richmond, VA | @tallestfriend @nicepassing

A person sits on a throne adorned with imagery of lions, holding a wand in her right hand and a blossoming bouquet in her left. A black tortoiseshell cat sits at her feet.

King of Wands

MODEL: Vincent O. Webb | he/him | Sandston, VA | @zorro_nova

A person sits on their throne, holding a wand in his right hand.

Ace of Cups

A hand is coming out of a puff of cloud, holding an overflowing cup. A hill is extending out from the sea with a rainbow in the colors of the pansexual flag.

Two of Cups

MODELS: Anays Torres | she/her | San Diego, CA | @anayst
Kathryn Frances | they/she | San Francisco, CA | @kthrynfrncs

Two people stand across from each other, holding up cups to cheers. A rainbow in the colors of the Philadelphia flag connects their cups. Above them is a black-and-white cat.

Three of Cups

MODELS: KNLH | she/her | USA
Kaiba Linthicum | he/they | Denver, CO | @sweetbabykaikai

Tenaya Jo | they/them | Oakland, CA | @totallytenaya

Three people are dancing in a circle, raising their cups in celebration. Behind all three is an arching rainbow in the original pride flag designed by Gilbert Baker, and the person on the far left is wearing clothing with the colors of the pansexual flag.

Four of Cups

MODEL: Ko S. | he/they | Oakland, CA | @blkdice777 @kodastrology

A person sits beneath a blossoming tree and appears to have a blank expression. He is unaware of the floating cup being presented to them, as well as the three cups at the bottom of the hill he is on.

Five of Cups

MODEL: Mai Ireland | they/them | Richmond, VA | @sideofbread

A person is looking down wearily at three overturned cups, completely disregarding the two upright cups behind them. In the distance is a bridge.

Six of Cups

Two children are in a castle courtyard surrounded by five cups filled with blooming flowers. The child on the left is handing the other child the sixth cup as a gesture of kindness. In the distance behind them an adult person is walking away.

Seven of Cups

MODEL: Tara Suess | she/her | Brooklyn, NY | @tarasuess

A person in shadow wears a polysexual flag shirt and looks toward seven cups filled with gifts, floating in a cloud in front of her. Some cups hold jewels and other treasures, but others hold curses such as a snake.

Eight of Cups

MODEL: V. Arias | she/her | Inland Empire, CA

Eight cups are in the foreground, with a person walking away from them toward rivers and mountains in the background. It is nighttime. The cups are arranged to show an empty space between two of them.

Nine of Cups

MODEL: Christien Seth Wills | they/them | Baltimore, MD | @critjen

A person sits comfortably on a bench in front of an arched and draped curtain, lined with nine cups. They are content and feeling fulfilled.

Ten of Cups

MODELS: Brandon Connolly & Mikayla Seaman Connolly | he/him & she/her | Idaho | @woughlfheart @sunrisewolfsong

Two partners stand under a progress flag rainbow of ten cups, looking out into the distance at their house on a hill and a flowing river. To their right two children are playing. Everyone is feeling fulfilled.

Page of Cups

MODEL: Ricardo Agraso | he/they | Caracas, Venezuela | @richiinavy29 @goldencard29

A person stands on the shore holding a cup in front of him. A fish pokes its head out from the cup, facing him. Swirls of the pansexual flag float in the sky behind them.

Knight of Cups

MODEL: Skylar Riley | they/them | Brooklyn, NY | @chocoboryder @skylar.riley.tattoos

A person rides on a white horse, holding a cup in front of them. They appear graceful and at ease on their horse. The background is barren except for the trans flag flowing out of the cup.

Queen of Cups

MODEL: Zoe Davis | she/her | Santa Cruz, CA | @zoe_nicole_

A person sits on a throne decorated with fish. She looks at the ornate cup in her hands. The cup is closed. There is a rainbow behind her throne.

King of Cups

MODEL: maya finoh | they/them | Brooklyn, NY (Occupied Lenape land) | @savagexfatty

A person wearing a robe sits on a throne. They are holding an open cup in one hand and a progress flag in the other. They are looking outward past the flag.

Ace of Swords

A hand appears through a white cloud carrying a sword. At the top of the sword sits a crown. Behind the hand, the sky is colored in like a wavy trans flag.

Two of Swords

MODEL: Eliana Rubin | she/her | Los Angeles, CA | @elianashirarubin

A person sits blindfolded on a slab with two swords crossed in front of her. Behind her is a body of water with islands scattered in it and the Gilbert Baker rainbow cut in half by the two swords.

Three of Swords

Three swords pierce through a heart in a stormy sky.

Four of Swords

MODEL: East | she/her/they | Oakland, CA | @theeastwesterner

A person lies on a bed with their hands folded in prayer position. Three swords hang above her, pointed at her, and one rests below them. Trans flag and non-binary flag colors are shown in the stained-glass window in the top right, along with a pink triangle.

Five of Swords

MODEL: Alyssa Lizardo | she/her | Spokane, WA | @alyssa.lizardo

A person has picked up three swords from the ground, with two remaining. The sky is frenzied with fast-moving clouds. Two figures are leaving the battleground in defeat.

Six of Swords

MODELS: Sara Neville & Jennie Eisenhower | she/her & she/her | Philadelphia, PA | @saranev @jennie_eis

A person rows a boat into the distance, toward a rainbow. Inside the boat are a woman and child huddled together, with six swords standing in front of them.

Seven of Swords

MODEL: STEFF | they/them | Brooklyn, New York | @ri0tb0ii

A person is sneaking away from a cluster of tents with two armfuls of swords, five in total. They look behind them toward two swords left behind, glad to have gotten away with most of the stash.

Eight of Swords

MODEL: Camille Leon (aka Allison Carvalho) | she/her | Chicago, IL | @camilleleonburlesque @allicwrites

A person stands bound and blindfolded, unable to move. On either side of her are swords, and there is a castle in the background.

Nine of Swords

MODEL: Maddy Wager | they/them | Los Angeles, CA | @madwages

A person is sitting up in bed, holding their head in their hands. Swords hang in the air behind their head, and they cannot sleep because too many nighttime scary thoughts are racing through their mind.

Ten of Swords

MODEL: James Manzano | any pronouns | Queens, NY | @james_manzano_ @j_manzano_habi

A person is lying face down, seemingly dead, with ten swords sticking out of their back. The landscape beyond the person appears dreamy. The cloth draped over the person is a traditional Ilocano woven cloth.

Page of Swords

MODEL: Mintzu Chen/陳岷慈 | they/them/他 | Brooklyn, NY | @_kintzugi

A person stands with their sword pointing upward. Their face is turned in the opposite direction of the sword. Swirls of the bisexual flag float in the sky behind them.

Knight of Swords

MODEL: Niko Nada | they/them | Oakland, CA | @spitswap

A person rides atop their horse against the headwinds of treacherous weather. They raise a sword above their head, pointed forward. In the sky, there are waves of the genderfluid flag.

Queen of Swords

MODEL: Amber Berkins | she/her | @withamber_

A person sits on a throne decorated with butterflies. She holds a sword in one hand, while the other is raised, inviting and open.

King of Swords

MODEL: Wes Graham | he/they | Brooklyn, NY | @kg_klondyke

A person sits serenely in a throne emblazoned with butterflies and crescent moons. The sky behind him is calm, and they are holding a sword upright and tilted to the left. A trans flag waves in the distance behind him.

Ace of Pentacles

A hand reaches out through a cloud, holding a coin in their hand. A Philadelphia flag rainbow shoots across the sky and into the distance.

Two of Pentacles

MODEL: Divya L. | she/her | Raleigh, NC | @divyalipscomb

A person is balancing two coins wrapped in an infinity symbol in her hands. There is a sea of waves behind her.

Three of Pentacles

MODELS: Fred Rivera | he/him | Canovanas, Puerto Rico | @EnriqueAragones

KB | they/them | Richmond, VA | @kaybbean

Nan Peña | she/her | Richmond, VA | @nanalela

A person stands on a bench with a hammer in his hand. He appears to be talking to the other two people, who are holding papers. The building is intricately designed and three coins appear in the engravings.

Four of Pentacles

MODEL: Madi Bowman | she/they | Orlando, FL | @shopwavyrainbow

A person sits on a stool, gripping a coin in her hand. On their head, they balance another coin. At her feet, she is stepping on two other coins. To their right, a genderqueer flag is raised.

Five of Pentacles

MODELS: Terri Meade | she/they | Marietta, OH | @tmeade0626
Clark Napasindayao | he/him | Fresno, CA | @arjunappy

Two people walk through the snow, minimally clothed. A bright stained-glass window shines behind them with five coins in it, along with a rainbow and a pink triangle, though they are looking the other way.

Six of Pentacles

MODELS: Madeline Graves | she/her/they/them | La Puente, CA | @monster_maddie_graves
Nico/Aura | he/him/she/her | @badaura777
Kyle Parker | he/him/she/her/they/them | Chicago, IL | @kyleparkr

A person stands holding a scale, handing out coins to the people at her feet. The two people at their feet appear to be asking for help.

Seven of Pentacles

MODEL: Adrian M | they/them | Sydney, NSW | @Adrian_alleles

A person is leaning on their gardening tool, looking over a crop they have grown. There are seven coins embedded in the crop. They appear fatigued.

Eight of Pentacles

MODEL: A.C. Williams | they/them | Asheville, NC | @thembo98

A person is working very carefully on eight coins, fully concentrating and focused on the task at hand.

Nine of Pentacles

MODEL: Marina Brock | she/her | Richmond, VA | @Brockstarhair
@Hifroend

A person stands in a beautiful garden. She holds a bird calmly in her hand, as her other hand rests on one of the coins. Eight other coins surround her.

Ten of Pentacles

MODELS: Talaya Banks | she/they | Denver, CO | @sunlightquartz

Mara Hasenstaub | she/her | Richmond, VA | @maragoose
Joe Gualtiere | he/him | New York, NY | @joegual

A person sits contentedly in the foreground, holding two coins. Behind them is a couple, with one of them holding a coin in their hands. Etched into the stone arch above them are a transgender symbol, a pink triangle, a labrys, bisexual triangles, the lambda sign, and the intersex flag.

Page of Pentacles

MODEL: Charissa Know | she/her | Singapore | @lucyintheskywithdivers

A person stands in a field holding up a coin. Beyond her are orchards and a plowed field. Swirls of the polysexual flag float in the sky.

Knight of Pentacles

MODEL: Asim | they/them/he/his | New York, NY | @zoomtarot

A person sits upon a horse, not moving, holding a coin in their hand. He is looking at the coin. An aromatic flag rainbow is in the sky.

Queen of Pentacles

MODEL: Camellia Jahanshahi | she/her | Montreal | @holy_matter_s

A person sits on a throne decorated with fruits. In her hand, she lovingly holds a coin. She is surrounded by luscious plants and appears content.

King of Pentacles

MODEL: Bug Cru | they/them | Coast Salish Territories, "Vancouver, BC" | @softworlds @bugtattoos

A person sits on a throne embellished with bulls. They are wearing and surrounded by an abundance of fruits. They hold a coin in one hand and a scepter in the other. A nonbinary flag flows behind them.

Acknowledgments

The *Queer Tarot* deck wouldn't be possible without our sweet and loving agent, Meg Thompson. Thank you, thank you, THANK YOU for always believing in us and our dream of spreading queer art across the world! You are so awe-inspiring in everything you do and we only can dream of being as cool as you someday.

To Shannon Fabricant, our amazing editor, for providing us with everything we could ever ask for in helping craft this beautiful deck and guidebook from the start, and for taking a chance with us and this project.

To Amber Berkins, our dear friend who helped shape our rough interpretations into something wonderful and cohesive, and for introducing us to tarot in the first place. For holding our hand and lending encouragement and critical feedback and for uplifting and hyping our dreams all the time, and for also posing in the deck! (Book a reading with her, you absolutely will not regret it! @withamber_)

To Jenna McBride, who fully put all trust into us when it came to designing the whole package and made the art and production process feel seamless.

To Alex Luciano, the Riso Queen, for teaching us everything you know about risograph printing, helping make our riso dreams come true with this wild neon deck, and for printing some of the cards and cover art for us.

To all the members and staff at Studio Two Three who spoke words of encouragement every day that we were pulling this whole project together and created a special and safe place for queers like us to make the art of our dreams, and for giving us access to the coveted S23 risos!

And the biggest thanks to all of the sweet and perfect queers who so kindly let us illustrate them as models for the deck. This project would be nothing without you and we appreciate you and your willingness to help us create something so big and queer and wonderful! Thanks to: Elsa G. aka Wild Black, Oran Colwell, Nic Charlie Perez, Rachel Brown, Leo, Nina Alexander, Jini Valence, Bailey Sell, Kevin August, Cassie Carrasco, Imani Russell, Rico Castillo, Maxx Rayne, Natasha R. Johnson, Toni Rowe, Riley M., Vincent O. Webb, Kathryn Frances, Anays Torres, KNLH, Tenaya Jo, Kaiba Linthicum, Ko S., Mai Ireland, Tara Suess, V. Arias, Christien

Seth Wills, Brandon Connolly, Mikayla Seaman Connolly, Ricardo Agraso, Skylar Riley, Zoe Davis, maya finoh, Eliana Rubin, East, Alyssa Lizardo, Sara Neville & Jennie Eisenhower, Chloe, STEFF, Camille Leon (aka Allison Carvalho), Maddy Wager, James Manzano, Niko Nada, Wes Graham, Divya L., Fred Rivera, KB, Nan Peña, Madi Bowman, Clark Napasindayao, Terri Meade, Nico/Aura, Madeline Graves, Kyle Parker, Adrian M, A.C. Williams, Marina Brock, Joe Gualtiere, Talaya Banks, Mara Hasenstaub, Charissa Kow, Asim, Camellia Jahanshahi, Bug Cru, Alett, Jul, Chala., jae, Taylor Tucker, Albert Rios, TK, Valentine Darling, Luz Miranda, pau venadito, Karli Miller, Danny Gee, Heather, Tara Shea Burke, Vico Ortiz, Eli Bird, Ricky Tyler, Jarred Daniels, Grace Duong, matty, Malek Ansari, Angie Cooper, Constance Shumaker, Danny Brito, Luis Miguel Sosa, Riylan M., Melody Lee Rosa, Edrian Pangilinan, Sofia Kon., Lee Ellen Fanning, Miranda, Mintzu Chen, Alex Teschel, and all the cats and dogs who also modeled for this deck.

Resources

Autostraddle article on queering the tarot, https://www.autostraddle.com/learn-how-the-tarot-can-be-just-as-queer-as-you-are-with-queering-the-tarot/

Ben Lucas two-hour learning the tarot video, https://www.youtube.com/watch?v=_NDuHfxp0NQ

Biddy Tarot, https://www.biddytarot.com/

Deck art examples, http://www.aeclectic.net/tarot/

List of Free Tarot Resources, https://www.reddit.com/r/Tarots/comments/25klnu/tarot_master_post_free_resources_for_learning/

Online Course—Jessica Dore (Meg's author), https://www.jessicadore.com/ecourses

Pamela Colman Smith history, https://enchantedlivingmagazine.com/divine-mystery-pamela-colman-smith/

Queers & Queens tarot deck, https://littleredtarot.com/product/queers-and-queens-tarot/

Queer Tarot: podcasts, interviews, queer spirituality & tarot resource, https://queertarot.cards/

Richmond—The Wandering Hermit, http://www.thewanderinghermit.com/x-tarot/index.htm

Rider-Waite deck history, https://tarot-heritage.com/history-4/the-rider-waite-smith-deck/

Roasting the Tarot—Major Arcana, https://humanparts.medium.com/a-review-of-the-rider-waite-tarot-the-major-arcana-b5ef5f201b6d

The World Spirit Tarot—2001, https://www.youtube.com/watch?v=wb_MEuficN4

With Amber: Readings & Card Pulls http://www.instagram.com/withamber_, https://withamber.org/servicedescriptions/